Max Landsberg is an author and business coach. Until recently he was partner at McKinsey & Company, responsible for helping consultants in the UK to develop their professional skills. He studied Physics at Cambridge, has an MBA from Stanford, and lives in London.

His books draw on twenty-five years of his counselling individuals, teams, and corporations; they have become best-sellers, available in fourteen languages.

The Tao of Coaching

Boost your effectiveness at work by inspiring and developing those around you. The classic handbook on 'how to coach'. Includes chapters on how to: *Give and receive feedback; Apply the power of questioning; Structure a coaching discussion; Create more time for yourself; and more.*

□ □ □

The Tao of Motivation

Inspire yourself and others. A guide to simple techniques and habits, to help you: *Feel and picture the success you want; Tap into your personal energies; Build your confidence, step-by-step; and more.*

□ □ □

The Tools of Leadership

How to build Vision, Inspiration and Momentum in the team you are leading or managing. Includes chapters on: *Culture and Trust ; Charisma and Power; Influence and Timing; and more.*

THE TOOLS OF LEADERSHIP

VISION, INSPIRATION AND MOMENTUM

Max Landsberg

PROFILE BOOKS

For EKI

This paperback edition published in 2003 by
PROFILE BOOKS LTD
58A Hatton Garden
London ECIN 8LX
www.profilebooks.co.uk

First published by HarperCollins in 2000

3 5 7 9 10 8 6 4 2

Printed and bound in Great Britain by
Bookmarque Ltd, Croydon, Surrey

A CIP catalogue record for this book is available
from the British Library.

ISBN 1 86197 660 7

People make history, and not the other way around.
In periods where there is no leadership, society stands still.
Progress occurs when courageous, skilful leaders seize
the opportunity to change things for the better.

Harry S. Truman
(1884–1972)

Contents

PART 3 – OTHER TOOLS AND SKILLS

Introduction

A leader is a dealer in hope.

Napoleon

People are often led to causes and often become committed to great ideas through persons who personify those ideas. They have to find the embodiment of the idea in flesh and blood to commit themselves to it.

Martin Luther King

In bite-sized chapters, this book presents techniques that will help you to lead a group, a team or an organisation. These are techniques you can actually learn and apply; I do not believe that leadership is primarily a charisma contest!

It follows the same format as my other books (on Coaching and Motivation). The format seems to work since the books have sold over a hundred thousand copies in fourteen languages. Specifically, each chapter focuses on a distinct technique for leading, describes it concisely, and illustrates how to apply it – using an episode in the dramatic life of Alex as he struggles to turn around an ailing advertising agency.

The book's central theme, which I amplify below, is that:

Leadership = Vision × Inspiration × Momentum

□ □ □

Like most authors, I wrote this book because I wished someone had already written it. I had left my role as a partner at McKinsey & Company, to set up an executive coaching practice. But I was unable to find many books on leadership that I could recommend to my clients.

Half of the existing volumes, outlining the prowess of famous generals and politicians, were fascinating to read but recounted events far too removed from daily life for the parallels to be convincing or applicable as lessons (New York ex-mayor Giuliani's *Leadership* is a welcome exception). Other books were typically arranged as workbooks with checklists to complete – and I assumed I was not alone in usually skipping over such exercises.

Thus I hope this book provides you with a refreshing view of the subject: focusing on leadership rather than leaders, and on the acquirable skills rather than on purely charisma or checklists.

However, I should warn you that this book does not ponder over *whether* leadership can be learned. I know it can be learned – in the last twenty-five years I have seen many people build the skills.

And I agree with Giuliani when he says, 'Leadership does not just happen. It is taught, learned, developed'; and with Michael Owen on footballers, 'I don't know whether footballers are born or made. But I do know that the more I practise, the better I become.'

□ □ □

But back to the central formula:

Leadership = Vision × Inspiration × Momentum

Anyone who personally engages with his or her team to create vision, inspiration and momentum will almost certainly be regarded as a leader. I have come to believe that these are the three most important skills of the leader. While personal attributes such as charisma may help you lead, leadership is ultimately not a charisma contest. The acquirable techniques are more important. (You may of course be perceived as having greater charisma if you habitually apply these techniques effectively.)

Now most of us have a strong suit. You might be better at the intellectual-cum-artistic skill of developing a vision, or the 'salesperson' skill of creating face-to-face inspiration, or the 'line manager' skill of sustaining momentum. But the challenge of leadership is to pass some minimum threshold on *all three* of these dimensions. That's why the terms are multiplied together – not merely added!

Part 1 of this book explains this central formula in more detail, and suggests ways for preparing to lead – e.g., if you are about to start a new project or a new role. Part 2 then devotes three chapters to each component of the formula. Part 3 addresses broader aspects of leadership such as delegation, timing, power, culture and developing your career as a leader.

In terms of format, this book portrays a dramatic 'true-to-life' story, summarising the relevant leadership technique at the end of each chapter. And woven through these chapters are several other themes:

1. **Leadership almost always involves initiating and driving change.** Nowadays, in a world of no *status quo*s, no leader can preside serenely over an organisation that he or she fails to develop. For example, while the leader may sometimes appear to act simply as a spokesman for his team or organisation, he or she rarely does this in the role of mere figurehead. Invariably the leader is using this role to build a shared vision, or inspiration, or momentum. Even when acting as a spokesperson, the leader is leading change.

2. **Leadership is a highly *creative* activity.** The leader is adept at encouraging the initiative and creativity of the other people in his or her organisation. But no leader can survive for long without generating his or her own ideas. The ideas may relate to relationships with the external marketplace, or to the organisation's internal processes or culture. Sadly, this aspect of leadership is often overlooked – and only the very best leaders explicitly set aside time for their own creative efforts.

3. **Leadership is an intrinsically *interpersonal* activity.** Effective leaders typically spend at least 80 per cent of their time actually talking to people. To accomplish this, they are extremely well organised and they delegate well – they do not allow administrative work to consume time better spent in face-to-face discussions.

4. **The leader is always more effective when the relevant people buy in to proposals.** Occasionally the leader does need to act

without having built a consensus beforehand. While this courage to go against the grain when needed is an important trait of the leader, this book focuses on the former more productive approach.

5. **Timing is important in developing a career as a leader.** Most successful leaders assert that they were lucky to be in the right place at the right time to take advantage of their particular brand of leadership skills. But in crediting their success to luck, they are probably being unduly humble. In reality, those who develop their skills as leaders tend to seek further opportunities to exercise those skills. Their career success usually stems from their courage in moving on voluntarily from 'good but undemanding' positions – to exercise leadership in ever-broader arenas.

□ □ □

We are all obliged to lead. Leadership is not the exclusive territory of the chief executive or army general. Each of us is placed in the position of having to lead *something* at *sometime*: we lead the family, the group of friends, the team at work, the small business, or the multinational corporation. In our world of increasing opportunities and our era that demands ever-greater personal initiative, leadership is a life-skill that we all need to develop if we are to fulfil our potential, and are to avoid the frustration of always dancing to someone else's tune.

I hope this book helps you to exercise leadership – so that you take initiatives in realms where you otherwise might merely have 'followed', or 'managed', or 'been managed'. Being an effective and responsible leader undoubtedly brings greater freedom and fulfilment. It almost certainly brings greater career success as well.

Max Landsberg
January, 2003

Despite possessing divine insight,
'The Mumblers' rarely pulled a crowd.

1 VIM: Vision, Inspiration and Momentum

In which Alex's perfect plan is tested

Alex was not enjoying his first day as Chief Executive of DKNU – the struggling advertising agency that he'd been brought in to rescue.

He should have been feeling more confident, of course. Having just turned thirty, having graduated near the top of his class at business school, and having been offered a senior role at the consumer products company where he'd spent the last eight years, he had reason to feel more assured.

But he'd left behind the security of working with his former employer. Lured by the prospect of casting off the shackles of large-company politics, he had jumped at the opportunity to run his own show. And as his friends all seemed to be starting their own Internet companies, Alex had felt this was the time to forsake security – in favour of adventure. He'd had enough of being managed by others, and now wanted to prove he could be a leader.

But now, as Doug – DKNU's Director of Client Services – continued his onslaught, Alex was starting to realise the enormity of the challenges that lay ahead. The advertising world seemed far less genteel than the industry Alex had just left.

'... and you call this a plan?' shouted Doug at last, waving the offending document. 'It's just an Excel spreadsheet wrapped up in fancy covers! This kind of stuff might have helped you rescue a consumer goods company, but it won't work in advertising. Advertising is a people business.'

Alex kept his cool. He held Doug's defiant gaze, and resisted the temptation to glance at the turnaround plan that he, Alex, had put together in the month since accepting his new job.

It had been as a peace offering that Alex had given Doug an advance copy of the plan. He'd known that Doug had secretly hoped to be appointed chief executive ~ and Alex had hoped that his confiding in Doug would help to establish a truce. The only other copy of the plan was with Sandra, the creative director.

'It's just a bunch of numbers,' insisted Doug, 'targets, ratios and deadlines. And nobody ever gave their heart and soul for a goddamn ratio. Painting by numbers might work, but not leading by numbers!'

'I appreciate your … uuh … frankness,' replied Alex, 'and I'll take on board your comments. But let's get one thing straight,' he continued firmly. 'I don't mind if you complain. I don't even mind if you shout. But next time you'd better have something construc- tive to add. We've got six months to make this agency viable. Six months at most! But I can't do it by myself, and nor can you. We're going to have to work together. So let's agree that we can both shout at each other, but only – only – if we've got something con- structive to say.'

□ □ □

After Doug had left, Alex drummed his fingers on his desk and pondered. He did expect trouble from his meeting later that after- noon with the wildly creative Sandra. But he hoped that Doug would be more receptive. Doug was in charge of the 'suits' – the account handlers who interacted directly with clients – and he was more used to the targets and management disciplines inherent in the turnaround plan.

Now, as Alex thought about the other directors, he wasn't sure *what* to expect any longer. Terry was in charge of Media – primar- ily buying airtime on TV and column-inches in magazines. Surely he'd be supportive when he saw the plan? Frank was in charge of Planning – market analyses and consumer research. Surely *he*'d be comfortable with the numbers and ratios? Luke was in charge of Traffic – ensuring that the various advertising campaigns wended their way through the other departments on time. How could he disagree?

But Alex was in for a surprise when he met with Sandra.

'I suppose it *might* work,' she said vaguely, after Alex had asked her about his plan.

'Really?' asked Alex, hardly daring to believe that he'd won the support of an influential director of the agency so quickly. 'So you think we can achieve these targets?'

'Oh I don't know about the targets,' she replied. 'We always leave these targets and numbers to the guys in finance. After all, digit stuff's for widget buffs.'

'But this is a plan to rescue the entire agency,' exclaimed Alex. 'And you're one of the most important people here … we can't do this without you … surely you've got *some* view on whether we can achieve these specific objectives?'

'Sorry, Alex – I'm really not sure. That plan is all about numbers, but the only way to really rescue this agency is with a breakthrough. A really creative campaign. One that will win some awards. In fact we need more resources, not less.'

□ □ □

Alex eventually gave up on the conversation, and returned to his office. He fished out his Palm Pilot and found the phone number for his former colleague and mentor, Michael.

Perhaps this plan does need more work, thought Alex, as he reached for the phone to seek Michael's advice. *Perhaps this plan is too much about numbers. Too much about managing, and not enough about leading … Not enough that's visionary and inspiring.*

But the phone rang before he could pick it up.

It was Steve, the Finance Director, on the line. 'The bankers just called. They want to meet with us. They want their loans repaid, even if it means closing us down.'

THE ESSENCE OF LEADERSHIP

The essence of leadership is the ability to create vision, inspiration and momentum in a group of people.

People are not led by plans and analysis. Rather, they are led by this trinity of other things. And the truly effective leader focuses nearly all his actions on creating them – using different skills for each element of the trinity.

1 **The *Vision* is a positive image of what the organisation could become, and the path towards that destination.** To create a shared vision, the leader is always hungry for novel ideas that fit with the organisation's strategy, and is smart enough to spot good ones. But crucially, he is also artistic enough to fashion those ideas into images and stories that are intriguing, meaningful and realisable.

2 ***Inspiration*, within the individuals that comprise the organisation, is what moves people to action.** The leader uses his interpersonal skills to excite his people, and helps them to see how they may themselves benefit from both the journey and the arrival. He helps them to see 'the word made flesh'.

3 ***Momentum*, of the organisation's projects and initiatives, is what carries the organisation to its destination.** Using his own energy and problem-solving skills, the leader keeps the mission on course.

It is on all three of these dimensions that true leaders deliver strongly. The visionary is not a leader if he cannot also inspire. The momentum-sustainer is not a leader if he cannot create a shared vision.

So, for small teams as well as for large corporations:

$$\text{Leadership} = \text{Vision} \times \text{Inspiration} \times \text{Momentum}$$

Of this trinity, it is the leader's ability to create a shared vision and to inspire the organisation that most sets him apart from the 'manager', as we shall see.

VISION, INSPIRATION AND MOMENTUM

Effective leaders create substantial amounts of Vision, Inspiration and Momentum in their teams:

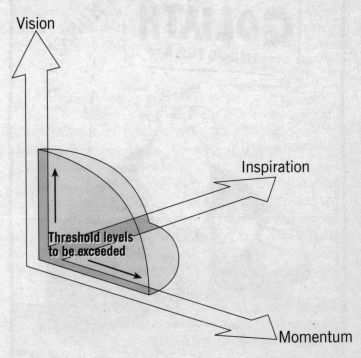

Note: effective leaders normally – though not always – start by developing a vision, subsequently addressing inspiration and momentum as well.

EXERCISE

Use appendix 1 to assess your current leadership profile, and the ways in which you will extend it.

*Until now the hostile bid for Dave's Slings 'n' Things
had been going pretty well ...*

2 The techniques of leadership

In which Alex distinguishes tools from traits

Later that day, Alex and Michael were talking earnestly over an evening drink. They'd known each other for four years, Michael had been Alex's unofficial mentor at the company where they had both worked. When Michael had asked how he was settling into his new role at the agency, Alex asked if they could meet to talk about it.

'So tell me about this plan of yours,' asked Michael.

'I've got six months to make the agency viable,' started Alex. 'After that we'll have run out of cash – simple as that. We have to get the revenues up, make the place a whole lot more efficient, and cut the costs.' Alex reached into his briefcase for his plan. 'There are ten key steps …'

'Forget the papers,' interrupted Michael. 'Just tell me what you're planning to do.'

'OK … during the last few years this agency has been losing more clients than it's been winning. It's also lost its creative edge. But it's an old-fashioned place – so they haven't reduced their costs or fired anyone. As a result, all their ratios are out of line with the industry norms. My turnaround plan focuses on getting them at least back on par. They need a 10 per cent increase in billings per account handler, and an average 10 per cent increase in output from each of the creative guys.

'I've calculated that I need to cut the costs by ten million pounds, and increase the sales so that the productivity of the creatives increases by 10 per cent. That's why I've called it the "ten-ten" plan.'

'But what's your concern?' asked Michael.

'I don't have a problem with the objectives I've set,' replied Alex. 'I'm pretty sure they're right. My problem is that everyone in the agency seems so reluctant to co-operate. I did expect resistance, but I also expected them to have more energy. I suppose I'm worried about whether I can get them excited.'

'Is that *really* your concern, Alex?'

Alex hesitated. 'I guess I'm wondering if I have what it takes to lead this company,' he admitted at last. 'Up till now in my career, I've been able to rely on a smart plan, disciplined deadlines and an energetic team. But this job needs something more – something like charisma. And I'm not sure I have enough of it.'

'It sounds like the main challenge is *leadership*, not *charisma*.'

'But surely they're related,' responded Alex.

'Yes, they're related,' replied Michael. 'But people tend to get very confused when they talk about leadership. They end up with a whole stew of ideas – some of which in reality are strongly related, and some of which are not.'

'Just give me the digestible version,' asked Alex.

'OK. Let's assume the leader knows what the overall objective for the company or team is. In your case, it's to rescue the agency. And you do have the basis of a strategy – you told me on the phone about the need to make the whole company more creative, rather than having the creativity reside purely in the creative department. And you mentioned several other things you could do – in addition to setting targets and deadlines.

'But now let's talk about leadership – and leadership is not all about personal traits such as charisma.

'If you think about it, there are several facets of leadership. First you have the things that the leader creates, in collaboration with others. Those things are a vision of what the company or team should become, inspiration within the people who need to effect the change (or who might need to design parts of the change programme), and momentum of the various initiatives required. You could call these three things "collective end products" if you like.

'The second aspect of leadership comprises the actions which the leader himself, or herself, takes to ensure that these end products are created. They are actions such as coming up with a draft of the vision, improving it through testing it with others, or encouraging people to take initiative, and dealing with the inevitable resistance to change. These actions are the "means to the ends". There are well-proven techniques for doing these things – and those techniques can be learned.

'The third aspect of leadership is the mix of personal traits that a leader has and uses – such as being charismatic, adventurous or principled. The list of ideal traits is a long one, and few leaders possess them all. But leadership is not a charisma contest,' continued Michael, 'and that's why you have to distinguish between these three aspects of leadership. You can try to change your personal traits if you want to – try to become more "charismatic". But you'll build your effectiveness as a leader much more quickly if you focus on putting into practice the techniques I mentioned.'

Alex thought he understood. 'I guess I've just been thinking about the business logic – and not enough about vision and inspiration. I've not thought enough about engaging people, because I felt insecure about my level of charisma. But you're saying that you don't need to have Nelson Mandela's level of charisma in order to be a leader?'

'Of course charisma helps,' replied Michael, 'but it's not the be-all and end-all, think techniques not traits. You don't have to rely on your genetic quota of charisma.'

They spent a few minutes talking about those techniques in more detail,* then Michael ended with a final suggestion. 'I don't want to worry you Alex, but I doubt whether your plans are as complete as you think they are. I know you're smart, but it feels like you're missing something. If you get people more involved in developing the plans – rather than purely forcing ideas on the agency – then you'll have a better chance of getting it right. Try talking to your clients.'

Alex looked at Michael wryly, then drained his glass.

---

*See the next two pages.

THINGS, TECHNIQUES AND TRAITS

Discussions on leadership often confuse three distinct topics: *1)* the things the leader creates, *2)* the techniques the leader employs to create those things, and *3)* the personal traits of the leader.

But the distinctions are important to recognise, if one is to build one's skills in leading.

1 Whatever the strategic and financial aims of the team or organisation, and whether his team is large or small, the leader must create vision, inspiration and momentum (as set out in chapter one). It is towards these ends that the leader acts; these are the **things** he creates.

2 To create vision, inspiration and momentum, the effective leader uses well-established **techniques**. It is on these techniques that this book focuses – these aspects of leadership *can* be learnt.

3 Quite separate from these techniques, the leader possesses ingrained personal **traits**. Here there is no magic formula – the potential list of 'ideal' traits is a long one; no leader is lucky enough to possess all the traits; and there is little agreement on those traits that are absolutely required. More importantly, it is doubtful whether an adult can radically change his ingrained traits – his time is better spent on mastering the proven techniques that are referred to above, and opposite.

The following chapters aim to support your exploration and learning of the techniques of leadership.

THE ANATOMY OF LEADERSHIP

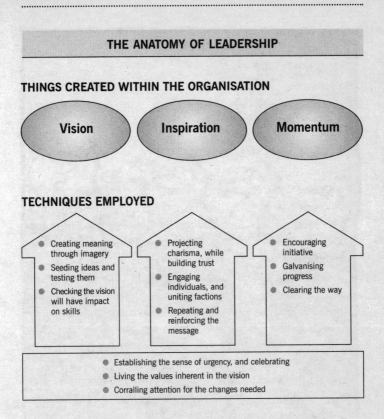

THINGS CREATED WITHIN THE ORGANISATION

Vision

Inspiration

Momentum

TECHNIQUES EMPLOYED

- Creating meaning through imagery
- Seeding ideas and testing them
- Checking the vision will have impact on skills

- Projecting charisma, while building trust
- Engaging individuals, and uniting factions
- Repeating and reinforcing the message

- Encouraging initiative
- Galvanising progress
- Clearing the way

- Establishing the sense of urgency, and celebrating
- Living the values inherent in the vision
- Corralling attention for the changes needed

TRAITS POSSESSED

Driven, Courageous, Engaging, Upbeat, Principled, Charismatic, etc. (See appendix 2.)

EXERCISE

Use appendix 1 to review your leadership profile and aspirations, if you have not already done so.

Once a year all government gene scientists are forced to watch
The Day Billy Forgot to Take his Hanky to the Gene Factory.

3 Preparing: focus, urgency and factions

In which Alex looks, listens and learns

As Friday drew to a close, Alex reflected on the endless meetings that had filled his first week at the agency.

Doug and the account directors had been insistent: 'We've just got to find new ways to keep the clients happy.'

Sandra and the creatives had been impassioned: 'We've just got to concentrate on great ads – it's more resources we need, not less.'

Frank and the guys from Planning had argued logically: 'It's the quality of the research and analysis that counts – we have to get more facts in front of the client.'

Luke and the Traffic controllers had been imploring: 'Everyone here has spaghetti diaries – it's impossible to fix a meeting. Sort that out so we can work as a team … for a change!'

And, of course, everyone had warned Alex against any attempt to impose timesheets in an effort to allocate time and costs to different activities. And they had also warned him to keep his hands off the collection of forty valuable paintings that the agency had acquired over the years – selling them would 'destroy morale … reek of asset-stripping … put clients to flight, thinking we're about to go bust'.

So the political factions were clear to Alex: each department was looking after its own interests.

Alex had also squeezed into his schedule a couple of meetings with clients. They had confirmed his belief that the agency needed to deliver more creativity to its clients. And it needed to do this with far less bureaucracy than it had done in the past.

'The planners are the root of the problem,' a client's marketing director had volunteered. 'For each of my advertising campaigns, I first have to talk to Doug or one of the account directors. Then he talks to the planners. Then the planners develop a brief for the creative department … then the creatives come up with something for Doug to show to me. There are too many links in that chain.

'Most of the advertising industry might still work that way,' the marketing director had continued. 'But it's not the way of the future. I want to talk directly with both an account director and a creative at the same time, right up front.'

□ □ □

This (and similar) comments had already convinced Alex that he was right to focus the agency on working in a more integrated way.

But, back in the office, Alex glanced at his overflowing diary for the following week, and knew he had to focus on his own initiatives too. He knew he couldn't come up with a complete, radically-focused, personal plan immediately, but he decided to start on it – to at least make the following week more manageable.

Obviously his role was to lead the agency's turnaround – but that didn't mean he'd be leading every initiative personally: he wouldn't have enough time for that. He jotted down his thoughts rapidly, under three headings.

His first heading was 'culture'. Under it he listed a few topics that he now knew required his personal attention – including 'teamwork', 'client focus' and 'innovation'. It would be these aspects of the agency he'd need to address in the more visionary and inspiring programme for change that he'd be developing.

His second heading was 'process'. Beneath it he jotted 'turnaround initiatives'. This was his shorthand for all the steps in the 'ten-ten' plan with which he'd arrived at the agency five days earlier. Even with his visionary programme, he'd still need to make sure that costs were cut. The bank would soon be demanding evidence of that.

His third heading was 'one-offs': big, substantive issues that might require his attention. He chewed his pencil. He didn't want to get dragged into operational details, but he felt sure there was something for this heading. Suddenly it hit him: 'pilot pitch' … he was going to personally lead the pitch to win a major client, using an approach that was radically better than the agency's normal approach: he'd personally drag both Doug and Sandra to the client meetings, as the client's marketing director had suggested. It might annoy Doug and Sandra, but it would quickly set the standards for the collaborative behaviour that Alex knew the agency needed.

It dawned on Alex that he would *not*, after all, be spending the majority of his time personally leading the initiatives that he'd so meticulously laid out in his 'ten-ten' turnaround plan. He'd need to find a lieutenant to lead that. Alex knew he would need to focus on 'culture' and the 'pilot pitch' instead. Glancing at his watch, he also knew he'd have work on those issues at the weekend.

□ □ □

Finally, Alex thought again about the people in his agency. He was amazed that there seemed to be no sense of urgency to change. There was a sense of an impending disaster, as word had leaked out about the agency's precarious financial position. But that had not translated into any appetite to adopt new approaches for creating campaigns or for working with clients.

He knew what to do about that – he'd persuade a group of clients' marketing directors and chief executives to address the whole agency … face-to-face. He was sure the meetings would have impact – he was certain that the clients would talk about how other agencies benefited from far closer co-operation between the various departments, as well as a few other themes that were forming in his mind.

'Kelly,' he called to his secretary, 'can you come in here? We need to rearrange my diary for next week.'

'I've just been quashing a rumour,' explained Kelly as she eventually arrived. 'The creatives think you're going to sell the art collection.'

'Next time you hear that rumour,' said Alex, 'just tell people not to worry. I'm going to take *very* good care of those pictures. Now let's sort out this diary. First, I'll need a meeting with Dirk van Allen on Sunday evening, if he can make that. See if he can meet here in the office. He's on my telephone list under "college contacts" …'

PREPARING: FOCUS, URGENCY, FACTIONS

The call to lead appears in many guises: on being hired to a new organisation, or on being promoted within an existing firm, or – from an existing role – on seeing that the organisation needs to be changed or transformed. But before diving in to wreak change, effective leaders first prepare carefully.

The extent of those preparations will clearly depend on the leader's familiarity with the organisation, and on the nature of the business issues to be addressed most urgently. But effective leaders always precede the launch of major changes with some period of looking, listening and learning. In doing so, the leader aims to answer three questions:

1   **Where to focus?** 'What are the priorities for the organisation or the team? What is the simple, 1-page, blueprint of the initiatives needed? Where will I invest my own scarce time? Should I focus on specific market-related issues, or on having people redesign the organisation's processes, or on transforming the organisation's culture?'*

2   **Now to convey and agree a sense of urgency?** 'How can I make the organisation see that maintaining the status quo is more dangerous than the leap it needs to make? What facts and proof must I marshal? How will I grab the organisation's attention, and focus it on the initiatives needed?'

3   **Which factions to take account of, and what coalitions to forge?** 'What are the alliances to use and counter? Who's in favour and who's against? What constellation of proponents should lead the various initiatives that will be needed? What signals will the organisation read into my choice of the team members?'

The effective leader continues to address these issues throughout the life of his mission. But he develops strong hypotheses about them early on – before he launches major initiatives in earnest.

---

*Appendix 3 (page 148) illustrates that the larger the organisation, the more the leader needs to focus on the organisation's processes and culture.

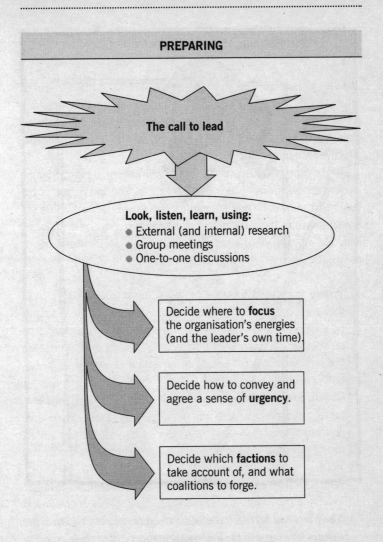

PREPARING

The call to lead

Look, listen, learn, using:
- External (and internal) research
- Group meetings
- One-to-one discussions

Decide where to **focus** the organisation's energies (and the leader's own time).

Decide how to convey and agree a sense of **urgency**.

Decide which **factions** to take account of, and what coalitions to forge.

EXERCISE

Review whether you have prepared sufficiently for the changes you are contemplating for your team or organisation – particularly in deciding where to focus your own time.

The Elves had never felt confident about beating the Giants at pole-vaulting, but the limbo dancing was still to come …

4 Shaping the teams

In which Alex picks people and grooves habits

The gabble of conversation subsided as Alex entered the large meeting room in which the agency's management committee met every Friday afternoon.

This was Alex's second such meeting, and he scanned around the table, checking that all his directors were present.

'Where's Frank?' asked Alex.

None of the other directors – Doug, Sandra, Steve, Luke and Terry had seen the planning director recently, though Steve said he'd seen him earlier in the day. All week, Alex had been trying to meet with Frank, but Frank had avoided him. Now Alex was wondering if Frank suspected the direction Alex planned for the agency.

'I'm glad we're *nearly* all here,' started Alex, passing out copies of his agenda. 'As you can see, I'd like us to address three topics today: the way we run these management meetings; my observations from various external meetings I've had this week; and a discussion about the changes we need to make to the agency. Any other topics we should be discussing?'

The others shook their heads.

'First,' said Alex, 'we have to realise that our mission as a team is to get this agency on to a stable footing. That's going to take more collaboration than in the past. And we're not just going to be a team when we're together at these weekly meetings – we'll have to find ways to retain that sense of teamwork during our day-to-day work.

'As a basis for that teamwork, we need to commit to some basic disciplines for these meetings. Here are my suggestions, but let's discuss them. First, I propose we meet on Monday mornings – we'll have more energy than on Friday afternoons. Second, let's commit to being punctual – we don't have time to waste if we're going to keep this agency afloat. Finally, I want us to keep track of what we've agreed to do: – actions, the various people responsible for the actions, and the deadlines we agree. We need just a simple list, not detailed minutes. I'll write up the action list from this meeting – but I suggest we take it in turns from then on. Any further thoughts?'

There was no immediate response from the others, so Alex paused – he wanted the others to be involved, and knew that someone would eventually fill the silence.

'How about confidentiality?' asked Steve, in his role as Finance Director. 'We'll be discussing some very sensitive issues … and in the past this group has sometimes leaked.'

The group spent a further five minutes discussing confidentiality, and other team disciplines to which they would commit. When they'd concluded, Alex called his secretary to track down Frank.

Alex next turned to the second item on the agenda – reporting back from the discussions he'd had during the preceding week. He told the group how he and Steve had met with the agency's bankers, and had succeeded in staving them off for a few weeks.

He also ran through a couple of pages he'd prepared, which showed data on the agency's declining position in the advertising market. But it was the findings from his face-to-face discussions with clients' marketing directors to which he lent most weight.

'I am now convinced,' said Alex, 'that we need to completely restructure the way we interact with our existing clients. I want us to establish much closer collaboration between the suits and the creatives, as we do that. We'll also need to overhaul the process we use for pitching to new clients.'

Alex waited for a response, but no one spoke. Doug looked uneasy, aware of the implicit criticism regarding his past management of clients. Sandra looked uncomfortable with the prospect of spending time outside her ivory tower of creativity. Frank – whose entire planning department was in danger of becoming obsolete – had still not arrived.

Alex broke the silence. 'I don't know how you ran these weekly meetings in the past,' he said. 'But we won't get anywhere unless we express our views candidly. If you disagree with what I say, then you must say so. If you have contributions, then you must make them. We can do this respectfully, but we don't have time to pussy-foot about.'

It was Doug who eventually broke the silence. In part, he wished he hadn't reacted so negatively to Alex's original plan two weeks earlier. He'd obviously provoked Alex into contemplating broader changes to the agency. But he also knew that the agency did need to move in the direction that Alex was indicating. 'I see what you're saying,' he said. 'But I think we need to talk about the details of how it might work.'

The group went on to discuss those details – though Alex indicated that it would be their *collective* responsibility as a group to flesh out the details during the following few weeks. Alex could see that Doug and Sandra weren't fully on-side, but he thought he could win them over eventually.

As the meeting ended, Alex recapped the immediate actions that they had agreed. Doug and Sandra would work together, to find ways for the account directors and the creatives to collaborate when pitching to potential clients. Steve would assemble a team to drive through the cost-saving measures. Luke and Terry would identify how the traffic and media areas could contribute to streamlining the agency. Everyone committed, somewhat reluctantly, to present his or her work the following week.

□ □ □

As the directors left the meeting, Alex felt he'd accomplished the first few steps towards forging them into a team. But he also felt that the action steps they'd agreed were still too piecemeal to present to the whole agency. He wanted to find something to make these initiatives more coherent – he knew he needed to develop a more comprehensive vision.

Alex's other concern was Frank. Apparently the director of planning had left the office for 'personal' reasons. *'Either he has a genuine personal crisis on his hands*, thought Alex, *or else he's showing the first signs of passive resistance …'*

SHAPING THE TEAMS

The effective leader confronts early on an important challenge: deciding what teams to establish and, specifically, whom to appoint to the team that will share with him the leadership of the organisation. He also decides which teams or groups (such as committees) to disband.

Ideally, he would have a clear view of the organisation's strategy and vision to help him with these decisions. In reality, however, the leader usually needs to establish some of the teams **before** the vision is fully articulated. Indeed, it is important that the primary leadership team feels that it has helped to create the vision. The leader is therefore inevitably confronted with a chicken-and-egg situation, and does his best to deal with it – some aspects of leadership are inevitably 'messy'.

Nevertheless, there is one aspect of the teams on which the leader cannot compromise: the teams' working approaches and disciplines. The facing page highlights constructive practices which the leader enforces in teams and working groups of which he is a member. These disciplines are of crucial importance because the way people work together in teams has such a huge impact on the organisation's culture more broadly. And they are as relevant for the leader of a small team as for the leader of a large corporation.

Finally, effective leaders usually find one or two special individuals to act as confidants. Though they may not be official members of teams, these are people with whom the leader can test ideas, and who can provide objective perspectives. The leader may need someone who can provide a 'grass roots' perspective from 'lower down' in the organisation. Or he may need a wise mentor with prior leadership experience to act as his coach.

TEAM HABITS

Good practices | *Ineffective practices*

Purposeful. The team has a clear and meaningful purpose, linked to the organisation's vision and strategy; objectives are understood by the team members and by relevant people outside it.

Unfocused. The team's purpose is blurred or out-of-date; or team members hold inconsistent views of the team's objectives.

Goal-oriented. Team members (and the team as a whole) know who has to produce what by when.

Procedural. The team 'goes through the motions' in a routine way, failing to deliver tangible impact.

Collaborative. Team members feel 'joint and several' accountability; there is a mutuality of interests.

Individualistic. The basis from which team members contribute is unclear, ego-driven or otherwise inappropriate.

Disciplined. Team behaviour is defined and enforced – e.g., punctuality, delivery on promises, respectful but forthright discussion.

Lax. The team has few norms; team members are late or absent; transgressions of norms go unchallenged.

Permeable. The team welcomes 'temporary' members when needed; communicates with the rest of the organisation.

Hermetic. The team is seen as a closed 'fraternity' or cabal; it issues edicts, but does not otherwise talk to the rest of the organisation.

EXERCISE

For a team or group you are leading, ask the participants to rate your collective performance against the characteristics listed above.

Nureyev might have co-operated if the last minute changes to his performance had come in more inspiring format.

5 Vision – creating meaning

In which Alex seeks a compelling image

The chequered flag fell to mark the end of Sunday's Monaco Grand Prix. 'OK,' said Alex, resting his hand on his wife's pregnant stomach, 'you win.' Alex had been sure that a Ferrari would finish first, but Sarah's bet on a Williams had been shrewder.

Alex retired to his study for a couple of hours' work on a coherent and exciting vision for the agency. He opened his briefcase to dig out his turnaround plan. But then he paused, and closed his case. *'Better to start with a blank sheet of paper,'* he thought.

He started with a logical, left-brained, approach – writing down the points that he felt his vision for the agency should reflect. Soon, however, he engaged right-brain thinking. He started to doodle and let his mind wander – just a bit. He knew he'd have to come up with a truly compelling image. And he wanted to impress the agency's creatives – not provoke their sniggers.

'What do we need: teamwork; collaboration? What's the problem: the "suits" just want to keep the clients "happy", the "creatives" just want to do great ads … to earn the accolades of their peers … the creatives never meet the clients. Everyone's just dashing about, with no time to talk to each other …

'It's like there's a great divide between the creatives and the suits. We need to close the gap. "Mind the Gap" as the tannoy warns us … perhaps I can use that somewhere.'

Alex searched for other images of the agency's great divide that he'd eventually need to close or bridge: *'… falling between two stools … the Great Rift Valley … the Dark Side of the Moon … tectonic plates moving in opposite directions … land masses drifting apart to create a stormy sea of confusion – How about that phrase which Churchill had invented: "An iron curtain has descended across the Continent"?'*

He thought more about the metaphor of East–West relations: *'dissidents eventually provoking glasnost – (I wonder if any of those creatives – perhaps some of the younger ones – would actually relish meeting a client occasionally, instead of being permanently cooped up in their ivory tower?)'* – His mind wandered off at a tangent: *'ivory tower – Tennyson's "Lady of Shalott" cooped up in the castle tower and only able to view the world through a mirror'* – but he picked up his pen, and forced himself back to the metaphor of East–West relations: *'– dissidents – glasnost – Reagan and Gorbachev – co-operation ONLY through the enormity of a challenge – space exploration – international space station …'*

Alex had only been working on the imagery for about fifteen minutes, but felt he was making progress. They didn't teach free-association at business school, but he found it was working for him. Draining his cup of coffee, he continued his quest.

Half an hour later he returned to the living room to rejoin Sarah. 'How's our baby?' he asked, as he sat down next to her.

'Fine,' she replied. 'How about your *other* baby – the agency?'

'It's having an identity crisis. But I think it's going to recover. Can I try out this idea on you? See what you think.

'You know about the main problem at the agency,' he continued, 'it's a lack of teamwork – mainly between the suits and the creatives, but also between the other departments. It's as if there's an iron curtain between them. But I want to portray the problem as brought about by the forces of chaos – something to do with an external Darth Vader … something that the agency can rally against …'

Alex spent ten minutes outlining his picture of the problem. Having favoured the imagery of the movie *Star Wars**, he explained the ways in which the agency needed to change. He portrayed the challenge they faced, the central role of the creative 'Force', and the fact that no one faction could succeed by itself.

'So it's not quite right yet?' asked Alex, seeing that Sarah was not convinced. Alex was more at home in the world of action than in the world of ideas, and he knew Sarah's marketing background and sharpness of wit would provide an incisive critique of his emerging imagery.

---

* Star Wars is a registered trademark of Lucasfilm Ltd.

'Well, I can see how you could turn it into something exciting,' said Sarah after a moment's thought. 'But it does need more work, to be really convincing.

'It is engaging, and memorable,' she continued, 'but if I were sitting in the audience as you unveil this, I'm not sure I'd know what to do differently. You kind of imply that I'd have to collaborate more – but I think you need to spell out more of the details. Also, are you sure they'll see this iron curtain between the suits and the creatives as a problem?'

'I'm pretty sure they'll listen when the agency's biggest clients tell them there's a problem – face-to-face. But I see what you mean about the vision needing more flesh and bones …'

□ □ □

Sunday evening found Alex in the agency, meeting with Dirk. He was one of Alex's old acquaintances, a possible client, and an expert on the marketing implications of the Internet.

As they concluded their discussion and put away the papers they'd been poring over, Dirk pointed to an uninspiring picture entitled *Grey on Grey*, which hung outside Alex's office. 'That's a Rothko, isn't it?' he asked.

'I'd forgotten you knew so much about paintings,' replied Alex. 'What do you think it's worth?'

'It's not in great condition,' said Dirk, examining it closely. 'Perhaps sixty thousand pounds? But I'd need to talk to a friend of mine for a more accurate valuation.'

'Sixty thousand', echoed Alex. Then he noticed the time. 'Hey – we'd better make a move. Sarah's expecting us to pick her up for dinner in twenty minutes.'

VISION

Few – if any – initiatives can be led without some vision of the destination and the route. The vision portrays the intended direction in an exciting way, and provides robust principles for responding to unexpected events.

If the leader cannot himself draft this vision, then he must seek help in doing so – but he must be passionate about what emerges.

CREATING MEANING FOR OTHERS

Picasso's view that 'art is an illusion which helps us see reality' is as pertinent to the vision for an organisation as it is to a painting or sculpture.

For if a vision is to guide a team or organisation, it must be a compelling story – one which portrays credible events: real people achieving a better tomorrow, in a way that the audience can emulate, and in a way that adds meaning to their lives. A vision is not just a snappy tag-line prepared by executives in group 'visioning' exercises, armed only with their thesauruses.

The opposite page suggests the hallmarks by which the truly compelling vision can be recognised.

□ □ □

The artistic skill to develop a vision is built only through practice based on emulating old masters, improving on predecessors, and experimenting. Appendix 4 (page 150) provides further guidelines to support your practising.

But the vision for an organisation is unlikely to be effective if it is the brainchild of only one parent. As we shall see, the vision usually serves its purpose better if it is developed collaboratively.

CREATING MEANING

HENRY FORD'S VISION

'I will build a motor car for the great multitude … it will be so low in price that no man making a good salary will be unable to own one and enjoy with his family the blessing of hours of pleasure in God's great open spaces …

'When I'm through, everybody will be able to afford one, and everyone will have one. The horse will have disappeared from our highways, the automobile will be taken for granted [and we will] give a large number of men employment at good wages.'

THE HALLMARKS OF A COMPELLING VISION

1 **A dynamic story** – not merely a 'snapshot' image

- Responsive to the organisation's history and needs
- Grounded in market facts, insights and foresight
- Offering a better tomorrow

2 **'Impressionistically complete'** – not an encyclopaedia

- Focused on specific changes needed
- Highlighting the priorities, and inclusive of the steps required
- Linkable to measurable goals

3 **Laden with meaning**

- Providing meaning to people's (work) lives, stimulating them to fulfil their potential
- Appealing to higher values

4 **Memorable**

- Novel in reframing or providing perspective
- Can be summarised in a short tag-line

EXERCISE

Sketch out a draft vision for your team or organisation *now*. Even if you don't need that vision immediately, your subconscious will improve it for when you *do* need it. If that is too daunting, draft a vision for some other group of which you are a member.

*Even as a youngster, Frankenstein wasn't
serious enough about his testing.*

6 Vision – seeding and testing

In which Alex flies kites and plants stakes

The following day, as Alex finished his meeting with Steve, the agency's Finance Director, he rued the fact that he'd chosen to start his week with a discussion of the agency's bank balance. Steve's projections indicated that they now had only five months before the agency became unacceptably overdrawn. Somehow, they'd just lost a month of leeway.

But Alex adopted a positive demeanour as he embarked on his two parallel agendas for the week. His first agenda, for the meetings that already crammed his diary, focused on the immediate cash-conserving initiatives inherent in his original turnaround plan. But now he wanted to add a second agenda to each of those pre-established meetings: he would test his emerging vision of the broader changes that the agency needed to make in its ways of working.

His first meeting was with Doug and two account directors. Alex started with the targets on which the turnaround plan was based. They talked about the allocation of responsibilities for current clients, and the ways in which they approached prospective clients. Then they turned to discuss briefly the forthcoming pitch for Surf-Earn.com. This Internet firm offered to pay customers large sums for using the service, rather than charging them for it. The firm was growing fast and most of the agency's competitors would also be trying to win the company as a client.

'What do the creatives say about this pitch?' asked Alex, looking at Doug. 'What have you discussed with Sandra and her team?'

'I'll try to catch Sandra tomorrow,' replied Doug.

'But Surf-Earn's holding the beauty parade at the end of next week – how on earth are you going to get the creative input in time?'

'That's Sandra's problem, not mine.'

'Let's get this clear, Doug. It's a problem for *all* of us. It's a problem for you, and it's a problem for Sandra, and it's a problem for me! There's been enough of this iron curtain stuff. This agency's going belly-up if the suits and creatives sit in their own ivory towers and keep pointing their nuclear missiles at each other.'

'I absolutely agree,' replied Doug, 'but you try convincing Sandra of that!'

'There you go again!' said Alex, swiftly conscious that Doug's account directors were looking on and starting to wriggle with embarrassment at the prospect of a full-scale argument.

But Alex switched tack, and adopted a quieter tone as he turned to include the account directors in the discussion. 'Probably you're all thinking "the agency's always worked this way, and the whole advertising world has worked this way – division of responsibilities for creative input and account handling".'

'But the world's moved on. We can't be having these stand-offs between the commercial account directors of the West, and the inscrutable creatives of the East …' Alex went on to explain his emerging vision of how the agency would need to operate in the future, stressing the importance of teamwork, collaboration and initiative. He also tried to make his vision more tangible, by illustrating how the agency would need to change the way it 'pitched' to new clients – having a creative as well as an account director at the meetings with clients, for example.

It took some cajoling, but Alex eventually got the account directors to open up, and to offer further ideas for how they might get the vision to work in practice.

But Alex knew they were only paying him lip-service – he knew it was time to up the stakes. 'I'm glad you guys agree,' said Alex, 'because we're going to use this new approach for the pitch to Surf-Earn.com.' The account directors tried to hide their groans at what they presumed would involve a lot more work.

'And by the way,' continued Alex, 'I think it's time I led a pitch. Doug, why don't I lead this one? We could use it as a role-model for how we're going to work with *all* our clients …'

Alex's day continued with meeting Sandra and the creatives,

Frank and the planners, and Luke and the traffic guys. In between those discussions, he talked with new recruits and old hands. Seniors and juniors. Thinkers as well as doers.

In all his meetings, Alex tried out various parts of his *Star Wars* vision – even incorporating ideas that had come up during the course of the day. In some of the meetings, Alex talked a lot. In other meetings he mostly listened.

By the end of the day, Alex had ideas with which he could improve and sharpen the vision. And executives across the agency were on notice that Alex was really going to change the way they worked. *Guess what*, were the whispers on the office grapevine, *he's even going to lead the pitch to Surf-Earn. I guess he must really believe in this new approach*.

□ □ □

It was eight in the evening as Alex paced back to his office, past Rothko's *Grey on Grey*. He turned right, and headed down the corridor to Steve's office. The finance department was deserted, apart from Steve who was still hammering away at his PC.

'I've just had an idea,' said Alex. 'What would you say if I could find us a million pounds over the next five months?'

SEEDING IDEAS, AND CULTIVATING THEM

At some early point, the leader will start to have hypotheses about the steps his team or organisation needs to take. These steps may constitute a prototype vision, or they may still be an unconsolidated list of action points. He may have developed these himself, or a working group may have assisted him.

Nevertheless, he now embarks on an intensive journey, similar to that of a politician before an election. In talking with many people up and down the organisation, he:

- 'Seeds' his ideas of what needs to happen
- Obtains further input from relevant people
- Identifies potential supporters and resisters
- Tries to (re)fashion the points into a convincing vision

The leader takes all opportunities to 'sell' the emerging prototype of his vision, while gaining further input from others. He may set up specific meetings to do this, but more frequently he merely takes 10–20 minutes at the end of meetings already established for other purposes.

In addition, he often pays little regard to hierarchies, talking with whoever he wishes, whenever the opportunities arise – as illustrated on the following page.

REFINING THE EMERGING VISION

EXAMPLE

The new leader of a law firm with 40 partners, 200 associates and 80 support staff decided the culture needed to change. As the firm had grown rapidly, various processes were groaning under the strain. He also felt the lawyers (including the partners) were not doing enough to become well known outside the firm.

He was about to launch the themes of 'Accountability' and 'External perspective', and tested these ideas with a broad range of the firm's lawyers and support staff, as illustrated in the chart below.

But his discussions led him to amend his agenda for change. For he found that the processes were groaning in part because fewer people knew each other in the now enlarged firm. He also realised that the lack of external perspective was linked to waning leadership skills within the growing cadre of partners. So, to 'Accountability' and 'External perspective', he added the themes of 'Personalisation' and 'Leadership'. Someone with a flair for marketing rearranged the initial letters of these themes – his change plan became 'LEAP'.

Leader's route in refining the vision

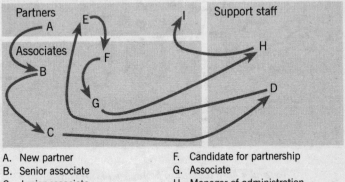

A. New partner	F. Candidate for partnership
B. Senior associate	G. Associate
C. Junior associate	H. Manager of administration
D. Own secretary	I. Partners' meeting
E. Mid-tenure partner	

EXERCISE

List the people to whom you will sell your hypotheses, and from whom you will gain input.

*Groc and Tharg wanted to be Internet millionaires
but Nunga was more realistic.*

7 Vision – sculpting skills

In which Alex checks that his vision makes sense

As the week progressed, Alex started to realise that his original 'turnaround' plan was merely a 'housekeeping' plan. It might stem the financial haemorrhaging, but only radically new ways of working could underwrite the agency's longer-term future. Alex's earlier attempts to make his original plan 'a bit more inspiring' would need to become a wholehearted crusade to reinvent the agency.

Of course, he could not ignore his original cost-focused plan, but he knew he'd need to invest more of his time on turning his other more visionary ideas into reality. And that meant spending less time on other issues. So he decided that Steve should lead the housekeeping plan – primarily because of his expertise as finance director, but also because he seemed to have leadership potential that had not been fully tapped.

Alex fished out from his briefcase the notes he'd previously made about focusing his own time. He'd dealt with the housekeeping plan, which had been under the heading of 'process'. The next heading was 'culture'. Alex crossed the word out, replacing it with '*Star Wars* vision'. That's where he'd be spending his time over the next few months.

Of course, there was also the third heading 'one-offs', under which he'd previously jotted 'pilot pitch'. Those words he replaced with 'Surf-Earn.com'. And that's where he'd be spending time during the next week. The pitch for the new business offered him the chance to build his credibility in the eyes of the agency. But – more importantly – it was the opportunity to provide a showcase example of important new ways of working.

As he thought again about his vision for the agency, Alex recalled a conversation he'd had with Michael, his former mentor, a few days earlier. Michael had advised him to check that his vision explicitly addressed the overall skills that the agency needed to develop.

Based on his previous experience in marketing, and confirmed by his recent discussions, Alex noted down the things at which the agency needed to excel.

First was the skill of developing true insight into the markets in which the agency's clients operated – and foresight about how the clients' markets might evolve. Only by developing and applying the skill could the agency hope to deliver advertising campaigns that had impact. Alex had seen little sign of that skill in the agency, so far.

Second was the skill of rapidly developing practical prototypes of creative ideas for clients – having the agency's people truly collaborate with each other, quickly assess whether their ideas would work in practice, and avoid individuals becoming entrenched in their opinions.

Third was the ability to interact superbly with clients – from the initial meeting, through to the delivery of the client's advertising campaign.

As Alex noted down these skills, he reviewed how well his draft vision illustrated the themes. For example, he checked that he could illustrate 'superb interaction with the client' by examples of how client meetings would include creatives as well as account directors.

Alex realised that he'd need to work further on his vision, for he wanted more than a simple buy-in when he launched it. He wanted a catalytic impact. He wanted the initial launch of the vision to create a cascade effect. People had to be capable of seeing the direction, then invent for themselves the details for their own spheres of work.

The creatives and account directors would need to invent their *own* initiatives, to flesh out the vision. The traffic co-ordinators and media buyers would need to establish new forums for discussion together, or build new workflows. In theory, Alex's vision could have tried to specify all these things. But in practice he knew that would be impossible – and indeed risked alienating people by being too prescriptive.

But he'd soon need to launch his vision to the agency. And so he needed to test it quickly. Even though it was not yet complete, he wanted to know whether his *Star Wars* theme would work. As an acid test, he decided to ask Kelly for her opinion. She could bring the perspective of an 'ordinary' member of the agency's staff.

'You've heard me talk about the *Star Wars* plan,' he started. 'But before I launch it to the whole agency, I'd really appreciate your honest input – *does it make sense, is it detailed enough, could it be misinterpreted?* That kind of thing.'

Kelly needed some encouragement to speak her mind, but eventually opened up. 'I'll be honest,' she said at last. 'I'm not sure about this name "Star Wars". The account directors think they're stars – and so do the creatives. So when you talk about "Star Wars", it sounds like there's a war between those two groups of people – not a battle between the agency and external forces of chaos!'

'I see what you're saying …' replied Alex. 'I obviously missed that angle. OK, Kelly, is there anything else? Please be frank.'

'No, I think that's all.'

'Come on Kelly – I can see you're holding back.'

'Well … uuh … do you *really* think this new approach will work, even if you change the name from "Star Wars"?'

'Of course I do,' replied Alex.

'It's just that you don't sound entirely convinced, perhaps you could make it more personal – something to show how much you care about the agency and the new approach?'

Glad that he'd bothered to ask Kelly for her opinion, Alex decided to test his vision on a few other people. He was starting to realise it might need radical changes …

CHECKING FOR IMPACT THROUGH SKILLS

So far, the leader has been crafting and 'soft-selling' his vision. But he will soon launch his visionary programme for change more definitively into the organisation.

As a final check, the effective leader tests that the vision portrays clearly enough the organisation's required skills (see the facing page).

In addition, the leader checks that the vision will be a catalyst for a constructive chain reaction throughout the organisation. He tests that his vision will move people to action, and stimulate a cascade of support. The leader asks:

1   **Will people know what to do? Will they:**
  - Understand the overall proposals?
  - 'Automatically' be able to imagine their role in effecting change?

2   **Will they be eager to participate? Will they:**
  - See the benefits to themselves, personally?
  - See the personal costs (especially temporary extra workloads) in appropriate perspective?
  - Derive additional meaning for their work?

3   **Will they be able to 'sell' the idea to others – without distorting it? Will they:**
  - Recognise the positive intent behind the changes needed?
  - See the message as simple and unambiguous?

cat'alsyst, n. That which aids a change in other bodies, without itself undergoing change.

VISION, SKILLS AND THE '7S'S

There are seven important aspects of any organisation – of which the organisation's aggregate skills provide the crucial link between strategy and other aspects of the organisation:

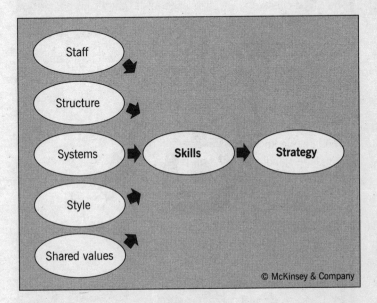

Note that the skills of the *organisation* are not merely the sum of the individuals' skills. For example, four virtuoso musicians will not necessarily make an outstanding quartet.

EXERCISE

List collective skills that are most important to your organisation (or team). Identify ways to build those skills – through different staffing, structures, systems and processes, style and shared values.

15 March 44 AD, and Caesar makes a serious fashion mistake …

8 Inspiration – building trust

In which Alex reveals his vision and himself

Only once before had Alex seen the entire agency gathered together – that had been three weeks earlier, when he had first introduced himself to everyone.

Now he looked out again at the sea of seventy expectant faces. He could just discern the shades of their emotions. Some nervously expected the announcement of redundancies, others anticipated a new Messiah who would save them, and the cynical ones were smugly waiting for him to put a foot wrong. But Alex fortified himself with the thought that all those emotions, deep down, were merely shades of the same colour. And that colour was hope.

Alex had worked all weekend to improve the presentation that would launch the vision of the new ways of working. As he started, the spotlights were on full beam.

'I want to tell you a story,' he started. 'Or rather, I want to show you a story …'

Alex clicked the remote control, to dim the lights and activate the video-player. A murmur of surprise rippled through the audience as the black and white images appeared. This was clearly a family video – and an old one at that.

The projected images showed children at play. They were about seven years old, and having fun. An adult had evidently organised a tug-of-war, and the children were old enough to relish the competition. A further murmur from the audience showed that it had recognised, from a close-up shot, the face of Alex when younger.

The two teams strained at the rope, and at first Alex's team appeared to be winning. But then someone at the back of his team leant forward and flicked the ear of the child in front. They started to squabble, and Alex's team was now short of two tuggers. The others on his side were soon pulled over the line that spelt their losing the game.

The next video clip was shorter, and merely showed a game of football in which the team advanced with a quick succession of passes. Though the fifteen-year-old Alex did not score the winning goal, his team did cover the length of the field in one sequence of deft and creative teamwork.

'Teamwork and collaboration and initiative,' continued Alex. 'It is teamwork and collaboration and the taking of bold, imaginative initiatives by each of us – by *each* of us – that will be the basis of our connective success. And to illustrate this point, I want to show you some video clips of what our clients are saying about us …'

The video sequence started with a shot of a meeting room, in which several of the agency's account directors and creatives sat around a large table with a handful of the agency's clients – and with several marketing directors who had decided not to use the agency's services.

The sound-bites struck home, as Alex watched his audience react to the clients' frankness:

'The world's moved on, but the advertising industry has not kept up …'

'Agencies *were* creative, but now most of them just shoot ads …'

'The markets have forced most of your clients to discover what teamwork *really* means. For some reason, this has not happened to agencies. That's why most clients are now actually more creative than their agencies …'

'You guys call yourself innovative, but you really have no idea what you're doing – your left hand doesn't know what your right hand is doing – your logical "suits" and your emotional "creatives" seem to be at tangents most of the time. It's not just you guys – most agencies are like this. But whoever fixes that problem can probably at least win me as a client …'

'Individually, you guys at DKNU have great ideas – but collectively, you have no synergy with each other. It's like you're a bunch of Oscar-winning film stars who can't even produce a B-rated movie. Come to think of it, you guys have negative synergy – if there is such a thing …'

Alex paused for the messages to sink in.

'The last speaker mentioned *stars*,' Alex reminded his listeners.

'I want you to think about those stars,' he continued, 'because we are all potentially stars. But at this present moment, we are caught in the dangerous gravitational field of another type of star – the black hole of financial distress.

'To escape with our lives, and to then write for our own futures the film-script for an Oscar performance, rather than a B-rated movie, we will need the power of collective action, and of team-work and of initiative. Only with this collaboration can our enter-prise advance at full warp speed. Only with this collaboration can we put this episode behind us, and go on to boldly explore new clients …'

Without pausing to explain, Alex ran his next video clip: a care-fully selected episode of *Star Trek**. He'd decided that the vision based on *Star WARS* just wasn't going to work.

'These are the voyages of the Starship Enterprise.
Its continuing mission: to explore new worlds,
to seek out new life and new civilisations,
to boldly go where no man has gone before!'

The opening scenes showed the Enterprise on a mission to make contact with a cyber-race that has the power of telepathic communication. But the evil Khan has finally caught up with them, from a previous episode, and has them locked in a force-field. That force-field is now inexorably funnelling the Enterprise and its crew towards the black hole, from which there can be no escape.

With all power down, only the logical Spock can save the crew. As a Vulcan, his resistance to radiation will allow him to survive just long enough to enter the heart of the thruster chamber, and there to re-load the di-lithium crystals which will power the ship. This he does, and the Enterprise escapes at full warp speed.

But Spock has taken too high a dose of radiation …

The episode continued with Spock's eventual rescue by Engi-neer Scott and Doctor McCoy. The evil Khan is out-smarted and

---

*Star Trek is a registered trademark of Paramount Pictures.

the Enterprise at last makes contact with the cyber-race ... to mutual benefit.

'Yes,' said Alex as the video concluded and the lights came up, 'life really *can* be like that. Sandra and Doug are going to tell you how – in a minute. But first let me share with you my thoughts on this episode.

'Initially, the Enterprise is doomed at the hands of the evil Khan. But who is this Khan, the evil one who has caught up with the crew? Who is this that has returned to haunt them?' Alex paused. 'Is not Khan the dark side of *ourselves*? Is he not the dark side of our own enterprise? Is he not the side of ourselves which – acting as an egomaniac – brings disaster through tunnelled vision and funnelled force-fields.

'And what of the di-lithium crystals which – potentially – can power the Enterprise at speeds faster than light, to escape disaster and then to explore new worlds? Are those crystals not the spirit of creativity? Are not the fission reactions the catalytic power of the creative process with which we are – or should be – working every day?

'And what of Spock's self-sacrifice? And the self-sacrifice of the other crew members as they endanger themselves to revive the irradiated Spock?' Alex paused again, but longer this time. 'Perhaps you're thinking that these are acts of pure altruism – giving yourself (or at least a part of yourself) for a higher cause? I think not. I prefer to think of these as the acts by which we define ourselves as real people. It is only through acts such as these that Spock can be Spock, and Bones can be Bones, and you can be you, and I can be me ...'

Alex continued, developing the themes of teamwork, collaboration and initiative. And he stressed that teamwork was not about submerging one's identity, but rather a way – perhaps the *only* way – to express it constructively.

'And lest anyone think I'm not totally committed to this new approach,' said Alex, 'I want you to know that I have accepted a very special invitation. Doug has kindly invited me' (*not quite an invitation*, he thought) 'to lead our pitch to Surf-Earn.com. Although our pitch will be a team event, and although we will *all* take credit for the success if we achieve it, I will take full responsibility for the new approach we'll be using when we meet with that target client in a few days' time.

'Over the next few months,' said Alex, 'we will he on a trek. It will be a trek that is to the stars … and for the stars … and by the stars … it won't be easy. But we can make it. I want you to join me.' Alex paused, and looked into the eyes of the agency.

'Now,' he concluded, 'I'd like to hand you over to Doug and Sandra, who'll take us through the new *Star Trek* initiatives we are launching, so that we can boldly go …'

To the surprise of the audience, the director of client services and the creative director mounted the stage together …

INSPIRATION

The leader has a vision that he believes will inspire others; he has tested it with a variety of people, and is now ready to launch it more widely. He addresses the second aspect of leadership: inspiration.

TRUST AND CHARISMA

Why should people bother to even listen to the leader – let alone to follow him? Why should they give their respect and labours to a leader, when in the short-term he can usually only offer 'blood, toil, tears and sweat'?

The answer is: we follow leaders because we *trust* them. As the chart opposite shows, people pay vastly more attention to whether they can trust the speaker than to the content of what the speaker says.

So the leader is effective only when he engenders trust in his team members, as the foundation for inspiring them. And he aims to build two types of trust – trust in his intentions, and trust in his abilities.

- **Intentions.** Being open – and showing what he is really like – is probably the most powerful way a leader can create trust in his intentions. If the leader is a 'closed book' and if people cannot 'read' him, then however smart his ideas, people will not willingly follow him. People cannot be led by a disembodied voice; openness, honesty and passionately expressed conviction have a better chance.

  And when the leader does open up, people tend to be more open with him – and respect the genuine interest he can then show for the things they care about.

- **Abilities.** Projecting well-founded optimism, realistic confidence and heroic conviction in the proposed way forward helps people to trust in the leader's abilities. To inspire others, the leader needs at least a modicum of genuine charisma. Stories and legends of the leader's prior successes also help, of course – but beware the overtly self-serving PR campaign.

THE IMPORTANCE OF TRUST

Trust accounts for at least half the reason for believing what someone says:

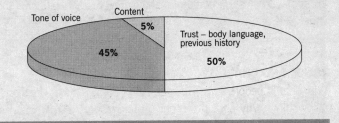

Creating, or laying the basis for, trust in you as a leader:
Building trust in your **intentions:**

- **Be open** – dare to show others what you *really* believe in.
- **Be consistent** in your interactions with individuals and towards the organisation in general. Avoid provoking 'It's not that I don't trust him – it's just that I don't know where he's coming from.'
- **Visibly demonstrate fairness** in making contentious decisions – the wisdom of Solomon?
- **Admit to your own Achilles' heel** or annoying character traits, and try to address them. Review Dale Carnegie's *How to Win Friends and Influence People* (excerpt in appendix 5).
- **Show you are serving others** (and/or a higher cause), as opposed to serving yourself.

Building trust in your **abilities:**

- **Exude appropriate confidence and optimism.**
- **Ensure your accomplishments are recognised** appropriately.

EXERCISE

Obtain feedback on how people view you. Decide whether their body language suggests that they trust what you are saying.

Before pancaking directly into the lions' enclosure, the 'Flying Gondalfo' makes a mental note to brush up on his teamworking skills.

9 Inspiration – engaging and uniting

In which Alex aims for commitment, but encounters a problem

Although Doug and Sandra weren't exactly holding hands as they took centre stage together, they did at least look like members of the same team. Reflecting on the effort he'd put into organising this double-act, Alex just hoped the cohesion would last.

During the previous few weeks, Alex had spent hours with Sandra and Doug. He knew that his most urgent task was to get Sandra's 'creatives' and Doug's 'suits' working more effectively together. But the two directors had seemed reluctant to embrace that idea, and had been unwilling to co-operate with each other. Alex knew he had to engage them, because both of them were highly able. They were 'high skill, but low will', so Alex had to convince them to join the cause.

It had not been easy. He'd started with lengthy sessions with each of them, over separate dinners, and had listened to them carefully. Sandra seemed more interested in ideas, the future, insights and novelty. If you talked about practicalities, the present, facts and utility, she'd tune out. But Doug was the exact opposite: he listened more to practicalities, the present, facts and utility. When you tried to talk about the longer-term future, or indulge in useful speculation, he would become irritated – to an extent that frustrated even Alex.

Eventually, Alex's diagnoses had allowed him to see what motivated these two people. Like everyone, they both wanted praise and respect and congratulation. But the accolades that Sandra most craved were actually her own: she longed to be able to stand back from what she had created, and marvel at her amazing artistry. At a pinch, Sandra might acknowledge the respect of others – but only if she felt their artistic skills to be at least as impressive as her own. Doug, in contrast, was more motivated by quantity than by quality. He was motivated by everyone else marvelling at his *biggest* billings, his biggest accounts, his longest unbroken record of serving a client.

As he moved to engage Sandra and Doug to his cause, Alex had built on this diagnosis. He had first helped them to understand the effects they had on people around them. Careful to include himself, he suggested that all three of them complete a questionnaire to profile their personalities: the Myers-Briggs type indicator.* Next, he had suggested that they all share their resulting personality profiles. This had not been difficult to achieve, because all three of them were quite 'proud' of their profiles. Then they had moved on to an increasingly frank discussion about how they interacted with each other – down to the nitty-gritty levels of how to conduct meetings in which Sandra hated agendas while Doug preferred sticking to them.

But in doing this, Alex had been forging something more important: a commitment to sharing. And they had at least seen a glimmer of how their differences might actually be complementary, rather than incompatible.

Alex now noticed that the audience was listening attentively as the duo performed their double-act: explaining the practicalities of the *Star Trek* plan. Doug and Sandra were taking the theme of creative collaboration, and showing how this new approach would be reflected in the agency's most important processes. In pitching to clients for new business, for example, the creatives and the suits would be working in teams together. And it would be these teams – not the agency's traditional departments – that would be the new powerhouses of the enterprise.

Scanning the sea of faces, Alex searched for Frank. As planning director, he had most to lose from these changes. The planning department had been the intermediary between the suits and the creatives – but that role was fast becoming redundant. Alex had talked to Frank about this, trying to show Frank how he and his six planners might apply their skills in either the creative area, or as account directors. Alex knew that most of Frank's planners could make the transition.

---

*See Briggs-Myers, *Gifts Differing* or Landsberg, *The Tao of Coaching*, page 36.

But such a move would clearly not excite Frank himself. It would mean Frank reporting either to Doug or to Sandra – people whom Frank had grown to consider as peers. Frank faced being demoted. His only option – if he wanted to stay with the agency – was to co-operate enthusiastically in making the changes happen. Alex had pointed out to Frank that this route was the best one for the agency, and the best one for Frank himself. It would be a chance for Frank to develop skills that the advertising industry would undoubtedly come to value even more than skills in planning.

Nevertheless, Alex was rapidly concluding that Frank was 'low will, low skill' – Frank was neither going to be willing nor able to make that transition. Frank's days were numbered, unless he could prove his enthusiasm for supporting the changes. Alex would be watching Frank closely in the coming few weeks – and was not surprised to see that he had positioned himself at the back of the room.

Half an hour later, Sandra and Doug had finished outlining how the new *Star Trek* approach would work in practice. Their explanations and endorsements had come across as genuine and uncoerced, and Alex shared in the applause.

But it was not going to be that simple ...

'I dunno,' muttered a media buyer to one of Sandra's creatives, afterwards in the corridor, 'it looked like a put-up job – what do you think?'

'I know what you mean,' replied the creative, '... but Sandra is pretty headstrong: she won't normally let her principles be bought. Perhaps there's something else going on here ...'

ENGAGING THE MASSES AND UNITING THE BARONS

'Lend me your ears,' the leader has so far asked, as he has promoted his vision for change.

But now he must insist, 'Pledge me your armouries', as he arrives at the moment of truth: the true launching of the programme for change.

Whether he is leading a small team (or leading a large corporation faced with the need for widespread change) there comes a point when the leader must truly gain the allegiance of certain key players. He must know that he has enrolled the relevant actors and agents to his cause.

Sometimes this is easily accomplished – when the key individuals are **both willing and able** to play their roles in effecting the proposed changes. In this case, the leader involves the individuals heavily, and delegates further action to them. (See box 1 on the opposite page.)

More often, however, the leader encounters pockets of resistance. In deciding how to proceed, the effective leader first diagnoses the apparent problem, then acts:

- If the relevant people are **willing** to help – **but not able** to do so – the leader will consider offering training or other support (see box 2 on the opposite page).
- Where people are **able** to lend important support to the leader – **but are not willing** to – the leader faces the more difficult task of convincing them (box 3), using one of the approaches set out opposite.
- If the people who will need to play certain crucial roles are **neither willing nor able** to support the leader, he will consider removing or replacing them – unless he considers it worth investing time in both convincing and training them (box 4).

ENGAGING – DIAGNOSIS AND ACTION

If individuals or groups are 'disengaged', the effective leader diagnoses the reason for this, and identifies appropriate action.

Diagnosis and action

Skill

1. High skill, high will **Involve and delegate** (and support in problem-solving, if absolutely needed)	3. High skill, low will **Convince** (see below)
2. Low skill, high will **Train or enable**	4. Low skill, low will **Replace** (or train and convince, if time permits)

Will

Options for *convincing* (box 3):

Engaging, 'pull'

- **Comment** – nudge people in the appropriate direction – e.g., using phrases like 'it has been noticed [by those in authority] that ...'
- **Model** – set a personal example
- **Appeal** – to noble aims or mutual benefits
- **Persuade** – through logic or vision
- **Negotiate** – with skill, courage and a tradeable 'currency'
- **Demand** – if you have the power, and if the demand is 'reasonable'
- **Threaten** (not recommended)

Heavy-handed, 'push'

It had been staring Lopez in the face all along:
half of them were rowing to a mambo rhythm.

10 Inspiration – repeating and reinforcing

In which Alex dramatises his themes

Alex had been waiting to pounce. In the few days after launching the new way of working, he'd expected signs that his message had been misheard, misunderstood or ignored. Despite the blatancy of the agency's need to become more effective, Alex knew that the pressures of the staff's daily work would soon diffuse the vision he had presented, and even eclipse it.

And so it was on to the agency's intranet that Alex eventually pounced. The 'suits' and the 'creatives' had come up with a simple plan for using the intranet during the early stages of developing new advertising campaigns. Alex had thought it a perfect example of the new collaborative approach, and was relieved that the idea had come from 'low down' in the organisation.

But the traffic co-ordinators were not so happy. They saw the thin edge of a threatening wedge. *From these intranet pages*, they muttered, *it's only a small step to a bigger system – one that will automate the whole traffic co-ordination job*. There was no way they wanted this intranet application to materialise, and Alex had picked up the rumour.

Alex blamed himself for not having spent enough time selling his vision personally to Luke, the traffic director. But he knew he now had to intervene visibly. It was a perfect opportunity to reinforce the 'collaboration' part of his vision.

He was tempted to call a meeting between Luke, Sandra and Doug – in which he'd give Luke a surprisingly tough time. But Alex thought better of it – instead he just mentioned, in every meeting during the next few days, how great an idea he thought the intranet application to be, and how it was a perfect example of what the agency needed. The message spread, swiftly.

And Alex had noticed another, unintended, effect. The suits and creatives had bonded perceptibly in the course of their frustrated dealings with the traffic co-ordinators! He knew he couldn't afford to let the traffic guys alienate themselves. Yet he was glad to see the emergence of the first pontoon that would eventually support the bridge across the great divide between the account directors and the creative department.

But Alex wanted to find more ways to reinforce the *Star Trek* programme for change. A discussion with Frank provided the opportunity. Alex had been trying, once again, to see whether Frank was going to contribute actively to the changes – or whether he was going to be an active (or passive) resister. For the last fifteen minutes, Frank had been promising support – but deep down Alex suspected that Frank was merely paying lip-service, to buy time for himself.

'Could I ask you a favour?' said Alex as their discussion drew to an inconclusive end. 'Could you spend half an hour thinking through some further steps we could take, to repeat and reinforce this programme?'

'I'm not quite with you ...' responded Frank. 'You mean like an article in the monthly newsletter?'

'Yes,' replied Alex, 'but there must be a whole range of other things we haven't thought of – things like using that intranet idea as an explicit example of collaboration and initiative.'

'You mean things like making changes in training and recruitment, for example?'

'That's right,' confirmed Alex. 'But try to make the list as long as possible. just include everything that people pay attention to – from the layout of the reception area to the layout of the telephone list.'

'I'll give it a go.'

'Thanks,' replied Alex. 'It's important, and I'd do it myself – but you've got more experience of the things that people notice around here.'

As Frank got up to leave, Kelly entered Alex's office. 'Are you all set for that pitch to Surf-Earn.com?' she asked.

'Yup,' replied Alex. 'I'm all set. Can you give Doug and Sandra a call, to check they're ready?'

'Are you sure Sandra's going with you?'

Alex looked at her inquiringly.

'It's just that I didn't think creatives normally went along to those pitches,' she explained. 'I thought it was just the account directors.'

'I'm sure Sandra is coming along,' confirmed Alex.

When Kelly had left his office, Alex buried his head in his hands. Kelly was the smartest secretary he'd ever worked with. But even she hadn't fully cottoned on yet? ...

REPEATING AND REINFORCING

As the diluting effect of the daily routine takes its toll, we often ignore or forget what we've been told. We even forget much of what the greatest leaders utter: from all of Martin Luther King's exceptional speeches, most of us merely remember that he had 'a dream'.

So the leader invariably needs to repeat and reinforce the message that conveys the substance of his vision. The challenge, of course, is to make those communications fresh and exciting each time.

While each team or organisation presents its own special challenges, the effective leader – competing vigorously for his audience's 'share of mind' – typically:

- Aims to gain market share of the informal 'grapevines' and 'corridor discussions', not just a share of official meeting time and memo space.
- Uses all available forums, not just especially-convened meetings; and plans carefully for questions from his audiences, recognising the value of those opportunities for expressing his message in novel and personalised ways.
- Finds ways to keep the message fresh and energising (the opposite page
provides an example).
- Perhaps most importantly, takes actions that highlight the new habits, style and values which the organisation is to adopt. Examples – such as making selective changes to the recruiting and training processes – appear in appendix 6.

A major pitfall is to under-communicate the vision. Especially in the hiatus between launching changes and seeing their first tangible results, it's tempting to tell oneself, 'I'll talk about this when we've made some real progress.' But unless the leader does something to keep the topic in people's minds, he risks rendering worthless all his preceding efforts.

REPHRASING

EXAMPLE OF KEEPING THE MESSAGE FRESH

When Jan Carlson took the helm at Scandinavian Airlines in the 1980s, he realised the need to dramatically upgrade customer service.

Although 'customer service' was a theme he promoted aggressively, the phrase became overused, and soon lost its impact.

Carlson brought intense and dramatic meaning back to the theme of customer service – especially for his counter staff and airline crews – when he devised and broadcast the notion of 'Moments of Truth'.

Employees came to realise that each time someone in the airline served a customer, it was a 'Moment of Truth'. It was a unique, dramatic and sacred moment in which service was to be delivered to the utmost – and in which the company's brand would be either burnished or tarnished.

EXERCISE

Review the communications strategy for your most important initiative. Use appendix 6 to identify further ways to reinforce your messages.

Badly-worded marketing.

11 **Momentum – encouraging initiative**

In which Alex builds a honeycomb

'I think we'll only need an hour for this,' said Alex, as he convened the fifth of his weekly management meetings. 'We'll start with any urgent news, then take a quick look at the financial accounts, and finish by covering progress on implementing the *Star Trek* plans. OK?'

The directors nodded.

'Well, I do have some news,' continued Alex. 'But I'm afraid it's not good. I heard this morning that a company called Megaquest.com has bid for Surf-Earn, our potential client. Megaquest.com is based in Seattle, and Bill Gates supposedly backs it, so the bid's almost bound to succeed. And Megaquest's agency world-wide is Cross & Rubicon, and has been for years. We all know what that means – I don't think we'll be winning last week's pitch.'

Given the work they'd all put into that pitch, the disappointment around the room was intense. Alex tried to dispel the sudden gloom. 'So, Doug, what other leads do we have?'

Doug covered the pitches on which they were currently working, but there were no dramatic surprises, so Alex asked Steve to run through the financial accounts. '*That should cheer them up a bit,*' he thought.

'Overall, our earnings and cash balance are in line with projections,' said Steve, 'apart from one exceptional item.' Steve gave them a moment to look through the figures, then continued. 'The exceptional item is a positive cash inflow of a quarter of a million pounds. That will buy us a few extra weeks of breathing space, but we'll still be hitting our absolute credit limits in just under four months' time.'

'So where did it come from – this exceptional item?' asked Doug.

Steve glanced at Alex. 'It's a rebate on some TV airtime we

bought,' he said. 'But we can't count on another credit like that one.'

Alex moved on swiftly to the final agenda item. 'In all our future management meetings,' he said, 'I want us to review momentum and progress on implementation. Steve will take us through the progress on the cost-cutting, and I'll take us through the *Star Trek* initiatives. Let's commit to each other that we'll do all the preparation for these reviews thoroughly. We can't waste our colleagues' time with sloppy work.'

Steve took five minutes to report on progress towards the deadlines for the cost-cutting, then handed over to Alex.

'Let's take a look at whether we're doing enough to encourage our people to take their own initiatives to flesh out and implement the *Star Trek* plan. In subsequent meetings, we'll also be checking that we're incorporating any early breakthroughs into our normal working practices, and overcoming any obstacles that appear.

'So let's talk about initiative,' continued Alex as he turned towards Sandra and Doug. 'That intranet idea your guys came up with is a perfect example – we need to encourage more of that kind of thing: high impact, virtually costless, and quick to implement. But what else is happening in your departments – and how can we encourage more initiative?'

Each of the directors volunteered ideas from their business areas, and Alex was swift to force decisions as to which ideas they would implement. 'This is a good slate of initiatives,' concluded Alex, 'but we need much more of this type of thinking – from everyone in the agency: from the receptionists, from the graphics designers, from the junior account directors. And I don't want us as a group to have to review all these ideas. I want people to just get on and do them; at most they can seek the approval of their departmental directors. But I don't want this turning into a bureaucracy.'

'Then we need to clarify some responsibilities,' said Sandra.

Everyone turned to stare at the creative director – she was the last person they expected to make that kind of demand.

'Take industry expertise as an example,' continued Sandra. 'Our clients and target clients in the banking industry have different needs from our customers in manufacturing, or telecoms. Some of the differences are subtle, but other differences are substantial.

'And we agreed that the agency needed to develop more insights into our clients' own industries. But our expertise in telecoms, for example, is dotted around all over the agency. The experts never talk to each other – the account directors who know about telecoms don't have a forum in which to talk with the creatives who also know about telecoms.'

The others nodded, but were surprised that Sandra was actually talking about *clients* for a change.

'It's like we're all bees making honey,' continued Sandra, 'but we don't have a honeycomb!'

'You mean we should have industry teams?' Doug clarified, in search of the tangible. 'Teams drawn from different parts of the agency?'

Everyone could see immediate benefits in the idea. *'Why didn't we do this years ago?'* they wondered.

But Frank could contain himself no longer. 'I think we need to be careful about rushing into this,' he said. 'Everyone in the agency will get confused. We're tearing up the old structure, and replacing it with all these teams. No one will know who's in charge of anything.'

Frank's colleagues looked at him in silence. *They* weren't confused by the idea – they could see precisely how the teams would be in charge of targeting and pursuing clients in specific industries. And they could see that would be far better than the current approach.

Alex decided to save Frank from death by silent stares. 'Let's just map it out now,' he said. 'It'll only take five minutes. We'll have a single page that maps out who's in which industry team. And at the bottom of the page we'll list the three or four results we expect from them. We're posting it on our intranet this afternoon … Sandra – this is a great idea.'

Reluctantly, Sandra accepted the praise from someone she still considered to be less creative than herself.

MOMENTUM

Even when the leader has inspired his organisation with a noble and laudable vision, he often notices a remarkable phenomenon – nothing is happening any differently!

In the words of Stanford Professor Jeffrey Pfeffer, 'How come everyone calls for change … but no one wants to do anything differently?'

The problem, of course, is not that the organisation has too little momentum – rather, it probably has too much momentum … but momentum in the wrong direction. The leader may have won hearts and minds, and pledges of armouries and resources – but now he needs to win actual arms and legs, as well. This is the third aspect of leadership.

ENCOURAGING PEOPLE TO TAKE INITIATIVE

To endow the team or organisation with momentum in the correct direction, the leader starts by encouraging people to take appropriate initiatives.

Tempting though it is immediately to use 'carrots and sticks' to obtain action, the effective leader should first check if any responsibilities need to be realigned. The leader of a large organisation may need to restructure reporting relationships, or establish new groups. In contrast, the leader of a smaller group might need merely to amend the accountabilities of specific individuals.

Either way, the leader changes the 'honeycomb' of responsibilities that defines the structure of his organisation. That done, the leader has four other tools to use – as indicated on the opposite page.

The 'appetite to take initiative' shapes the organisation's culture – and is also shaped by it. Because of its importance, the effective leader returns frequently to addressing the issue once he has taken other steps to build momentum.

ENCOURAGING INITIATIVE

1   **Change the 'honeycomb' of group responsibilities within the organisation (or of individual responsibilities within the team).** Ensure that the relevant objectives, resources and responsibilities are co-located. Help groups understand how they 'dovetail' together. Check that each group is well led and has a clear mission. Set up new groups and disband others, if needed.

2   **Install simple disciplines for action.** At the very least, develop a habit for meetings to conclude with a list of agreed actions, responsibilities and deadlines. If necessary, take the lead in providing a visible example – in meetings which you attend.

3   **Infiltrate.** Establish cross-functional teams, staffed with respected mavericks. These teams tend to develop their own initiative-oriented cultures – and can act as beach-heads into lethargic departments.

4   **Reward risk-taking.** For example, to show that risk-taking was legitimate, a major corporation promoted a manager who had taken a thoroughly analysed – yet eventually disastrous – risk. This promotion was risky for the corporation, but that very fact made the signal doubly powerful.

5   **Use carrot and stick.** Reward radical progress achieved through entrepreneurial initiative, and admonish (or punish) its absence. Consider using personal congratulation, public praise, promotion, pay.

EXERCISE

For the team or organisation that you are leading, identify which individuals (or groups) are action-oriented, and which are lethargic. Then take the appropriate action.

'Yes, very clever I'm sure Einstein, but in case you hadn't noticed ...
today's assignment is to make an explosion.'

12 **Momentum – galvanising progress**

In which Alex builds on some early successes

Kelly, can you show me how this goddamn system works?' asked Alex. 'I want to send a voicemail message to everyone in the agency.'

Kelly showed him the buttons to press, and Alex started reading the message from the bullet points he'd scrawled excitedly.

'This is Alex, with a message for everyone. As you know, we made a pitch to Surf-Earn.com three weeks ago. This was an important target client, and we were disappointed to learn – immediately after our pitch – that they were to be acquired by a company which only used Cross & Rubicon as their advertising agency. However, I've just talked with the chief executive of Surf-Earn.com, and I wanted to relay the news to you as quickly as possible – I'm glad to tell you that we have won the account.

'This win was in the face of intense competition – not only from Cross & Rubicon, but from many other agencies keen to serve this high profile company. Our success bears testimony to our new approach to teamwork – and specifically to the joint efforts of Sandra and Doug. The client specifically cited our novel approach as the reason they selected us. I wanted you all to know about this as soon as possible. Congratulations.'

Alex pressed #, and the message sped to seventy destinations simultaneously.

□□□

A few hours later, the directors convened for their weekly review of progress on the *Star Trek* initiative. 'I want to focus on galvanising progress,' started Alex.

'I don't like to seem illiterate,' interrupted Terry. 'But this word "galvanise" you keep using – what exactly do you mean?'

'Galvanise,' obliged Sandra, 'to rouse, stimulate or excite – as if by use of electric current or shock.' Sandra had started her career as a copywriter.

'Precisely,' confirmed Alex. 'Our role as a leadership team is to keep the agency roused and stimulated and excited. I'd prefer to avoid using electric shocks if possible, but our role is indeed to be the pacemakers – and not necessarily peacemakers!' His pun didn't even raise a smile from a group whose standard of word-play was high.

'So, in order to galvanise progress,' continued Alex, 'I want us to address three things: first, consolidating what we've achieved so far; second, creating more "early wins"; and third, identifying any further initiatives we need to launch.'

'Our biggest achievement so far was winning Surf-Earn,' said Doug. 'When you say "consolidate progress", I suppose you mean build the success formula into our everyday working practices? … Well, for a start, we could ensure we always do the quality of research that we put into that pitch.'

'But we do!' insisted Frank, protecting his planning team.

'We'll get nowhere if we're parochial and defensive,' interrupted Alex. 'We're going to improve every area of this agency – including my performance as chief executive. So go on, Doug: explain what you mean in practice.'

Doug listed a few ideas, and other directors chipped in, too. Some of the ideas sounded pedestrian, but probably made good sense – such as drawing up standard checklists for teams to use when they researched forthcoming pitches. Other ideas sounded more glamorous, but needed to be examined in more detail before they could be implemented – such as having a rapid-response team on standby at all times, ready to pitch to potential clients.

But in just twenty minutes, the group had identified several novel ideas that they decided to institute as 'normal practice' – ideas which had sprung out of the 'pilot pitch' to Surf-Earn.

Next, they reviewed the honeycomb of industry teams, which they'd set up several weeks earlier. But it was still too early to declare any victories in that area.

'So,' urged Alex, 'item two on the agenda: what other "early wins" can we aim for? Is there anything we can do to upgrade the way we serve existing clients? Or anything in other areas of the business? We're looking for ideas which are quick to implement, and which will encourage the agency by showing that the *Star Trek* approach really is working.'

'And it must be something that earns revenue or saves costs,' insisted Steve. 'Don't forget our cash flow.'

Alex again broached the subject of selling the art collection, but was confronted by unanimous dissent and near mutiny. There were just no other costs to attack – Alex's initial 'housekeeping' plan had covered everything. Determined that they come up with *something*, Alex made some minor suggestions, which the group endorsed.

Finally, they turned to identifying additional medium-term projects that would tie in with the *Star Trek* initiatives, but which would extend the themes more broadly throughout the agency. Alex hoped this would keep the agency's attention focused on the mission.

The newly-established industry teams appeared to provide a fruitful starting point. They talked about extending that initiative, by establishing a strategic project to decide more definitively which industry sectors to focus on. That would certainly reinforce the themes of industry insight as well as collaboration. And they were particularly keen to establish a group that would focus on Internet companies.

After discussing this strategic project, however, they decided to pursue it later. They felt the agency already had enough change to digest. And even their current plans weren't going to be plain sailing ...

GALVANISING PROGRESS

The leader and his collaborators have articulated an inspiring vision, and have taken the first steps to build momentum. But still there's not enough momentum. What's going wrong, and what does the leader do about it?

At this point, the momentum developed by the organisation is directly proportional to the 'momentum' of the leader and his immediate team. Effective leaders do not now reflect quietly, but instead spend most of their time with other people, face-to-face. To galvanise the efforts of others, and to build on initial progress, they:

- **Aim for 'early wins' and quick successes.** An example might be declaring the successful establishment (even if not the completion) of a pilot initiative that will form the basis of a subsequent rollout across the organisation. To declare such a success clearly requires that the leader – or a top management group – has formally reviewed progress. (And merely announcing the date of the review often strikes action into the hearts of the relevant managers.)

- **Consolidate progress, 'ratcheting' it into a *new modus operandi*.** The leader has the organisation develop new information systems, processes or structures (possibly only temporary ones), to quickly groove the team or organisation into the positive habits which it has started to develop.

- **Launch initiatives that reinforce the main mission.** For example, in a mission to improve the effectiveness of the salesforce, the leader may instigate additional projects that focus on salesforce remuneration, or coaching of new salespeople to improve their productivity and retention. By launching several appropriate initiatives, the leader gains greater 'air time' for his overall programme, and a larger share of managers' attention.

- **Identify lapses or relapses, and correct them.** In group meetings or in one-to-one discussion, the leader addresses issues of non-performance, using appropriate levels of tact or confrontation. The leader chooses his words carefully, to send important signals. For example, he uses phrases like 'we're interested in outputs, not inputs' with teams which are working hard but which are slow to arrive at recommendations.

A TYPICAL PROGRESSION

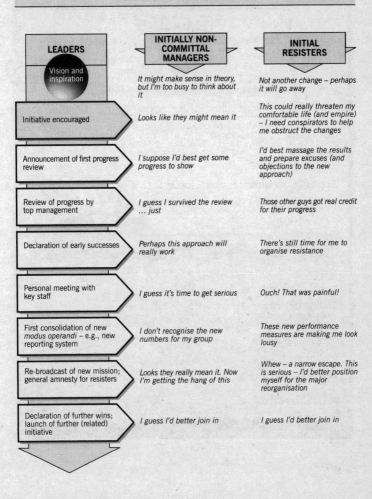

LEADERS	INITIALLY NON-COMMITTAL MANAGERS	INITIAL RESISTERS
Vision and inspiration	It might make sense in theory, but I'm too busy to think about it	Not another change – perhaps it will go away
Initiative encouraged	Looks like they might mean it	This could really threaten my comfortable life (and empire) – I need conspirators to help me obstruct the changes
Announcement of first progress review	I suppose I'd best get some progress to show	I'd best massage the results and prepare excuses (and objections to the new approach)
Review of progress by top management	I guess I survived the review … just	Those other guys got real credit for their progress
Declaration of early successes	Perhaps this approach will really work	There's still time for me to organise resistance
Personal meeting with key staff	I guess it's time to get serious	Ouch! That was painful!
First consolidation of new modus operandi – e.g., new reporting system	I don't recognise the new numbers for my group	These new performance measures are making me look lousy
Re-broadcast of new mission; general amnesty for resisters	Looks they really mean it. Now I'm getting the hang of this	Whew – a narrow escape. This is serious – I'd better position myself for the major reorganisation
Declaration of further wins; launch of further (related) initiative	I guess I'd better join in	I guess I'd better join in

EXERCISE

For a mission you are leading, sketch the initiatives you are using to galvanise progress.

13 **Momentum – clearing the way**

In which Alex tackles some roadblocks

During the following six weeks, the idea of forming a group to focus on the Internet industry had gradually gained approval across the agency.

With suggestions from his directors, Alex had assembled a relevant team. Doug had volunteered Len – one of his account directors – to lead the group. Sandra had endorsed the suggestion, and the team seemed ready to roll.

But ten days later, as Alex was waiting for the coffee machine to spill his coffee for him, he overheard a conversation that disturbed him. From around the corner, another account director had asked, 'So, Len, I hear you're in charge of this Internet team – how's it going?'

'I haven't had time to think about it – I'm working on a pitch to IBM.'

'Wow – IBM,' his colleague replied, 'I didn't know we might be working for them!'

'Doug's told me it's top priority,' replied Len. 'I've had to drop everything else – I'm working fifteen hours a day on it.'

'I bet you get lots of brownie points for working on that pitch.'

'Dead right,' confirmed Len. 'If we do get bonuses this year, I get big time credit for even preparing the pitch, let alone if we win it.' Alex heard Len continue in animated style, but he didn't hear Len mention another word about the Internet project!

A few minutes later, Alex was in Doug's office, with the door closed.

'We have a problem,' Alex started. 'It's about Len and the Internet project. I hear he's spending most of his time on the pitch for IBM. Is that right?'

'I don't think so,' replied Doug. 'I asked him to spend half of his time on IBM, and the other half on leading the Internet project.'

'I'll bet it's not working that way in practice, Doug. And we're not going to waste time in an unproductive meeting next time we review that project. Can you at least check he's got the team up and running?'

□ □ □

Doug got back to Alex later that day. He was apologetic, and admitted that Len had indeed accomplished little so far. When Alex pressed him for details, he conceded that Len had not yet even called a meeting of the team.

But Doug did defend Len, by pointing out that the incentive system for the account directors only rewarded time spent directly on client business.

'Then tell Len that this project is going to attract full credit,' said Alex. 'We're going to be having a few more of these projects in the future, so we'd better get this system amended. But in the meantime, tell him I've authorised the credit, personally.'

'OK,' said Doug, relieved that he'd escaped so easily.

'But that won't be enough, will it?' asked Alex.

'How d'you mean?' Doug's reply appeared innocent enough.

'Well, even with the amended system, Len's still going to think it's more important to work on winning a potential client.'

'I guess so …'

Alex considered his repertoire of ways to prise more of Len's time from Doug. *'Doug is able and willing to free up more of Len's time,'* thought Alex. *'He's high will and high skill – so he doesn't need me to PERSUADE him. The right path is "involve then delegate – but support through problem-solving, if needed".'*

'We all agreed that Len was the best person for the job,' started Alex. 'But if you can't convince him to free up the time, then we'll have to find another team leader. And that would be very bad news – I don't want the agency to see us doing a U-turn on the very first of these cross-department teams. That won't exactly build our credibility as a top management group, will it?'

Doug thought for a moment. On the one hand Alex was right, but on the other hand he really needed Len's help for the IBM pitch. It seemed like stalemate.

'How about that new person you just hired?' asked Alex.

'You mean Rachel?'

'That's right,' said Alex. 'She used to work for Microsoft – she must know about the Internet. Why not get her to take over from Len?'

'But Rachel doesn't have enough advertising background ...'

'I was one of the people who interviewed her,' countered Alex, 'and she seemed pretty knowledgeable to me. Why not get Len to spend just a third of his time on the Internet project, and have Rachel help him?'

Doug agreed reluctantly – though he'd planned for Rachel to work on another account.

'I'm looking forward to next week's review of the project ...' smiled Alex mischievously. 'It had better be good!'

□ □ □

But Alex was not smiling as he returned to his office. Deciding to change the bonus and credit system had been an easy way to clear away an obstacle to progress. It had merely required bending a misaligned process into the required shape.

Firing people was more painful, however. Yet Alex felt he had no choice. During the three months since joining the agency, Alex had been watching Frank closely, and it was now clear that he had become an obstacle that had to be addressed directly. He was setting a negative example for the six planners who reported to him, distracting people with his passive resistance to change, and generally dragging his heels. Alex picked up his phone, and called DKNU's employment lawyer.

CLEARING THE WAY

In building momentum, the obstacles that impede the organisation are typically *a)* misaligned processes, and *b)* unhelpful actions by certain managers and staff. The effective leader watches out for emerging obstacles, and takes personal (or indirect) action to deal with them swiftly.

- **Misaligned processes** are systems, procedures and ways of working that were appropriate for the old *modus operandi*, but not for the new one. In theory, problems of misalignment can be anticipated and pre-empted (as illustrated on the opposite page).
- **Unhelpful actions** by others include avoidance, passive resistance, and sometimes downright political sabotage. These obstacles are more difficult to foresee thoroughly, and are therefore more difficult to pre-empt.

    In addressing these problems, it is crucial to diagnose why the resister is avoiding change, and to assess the relative power and information that the leader and resisters possess. Only then can the leader adopt the appropriate strategy to win the rebels over.

    Though resistance may stem from hostility and ill-intention, it may have other origins – ones that are easier to address. These include: *a)* disagreement about (or misunderstanding of) any external market factors that are requiring the change, and *b)* misunderstanding about the benefits and costs of the changes to the individual, in terms of prestige, workload, etc.

    Revisit 'Engaging and Uniting' (chapter 9, page 51) and appendix 7, page 155 for techniques to address these obstacles.

MISALIGNED PROCESSES TO ANTICIPATE

Immediate/short term:

- **Weekly or monthly operational reports** to executives, managers and staff do not focus on (nor even reveal) the newly agreed 'key indicators of performance'.
- **New critical paths** for movements of information or materials do not mesh completely.
- **New, temporary, systems to monitor speed of implementation** are not 'learned' or are not used correctly.

Medium/longer term:

- **Performance measurement systems** for individuals and/or divisions remain focused on outdated criteria.
- **New forums for making decisions** (especially 'cross-functional' ones) are not established, are staffed with inappropriate people, fail to receive or produce required work, or develop dysfunctional habits in their infancy.
- **Hiring and promotion decisions** send signals that contradict the new values or approach.

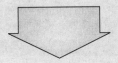

There are clear merits to anticipating these problems and pre-empting them. The most important process issues should be addressed early, while 'fleshing out' the vision.

For example: if revamping the salesforce, the leader or his team can dramatically caricature the new 'ideal salesman' or 'ideal sales manager' – *and ensure this image stays with the appropriate implementation teams*. This will be a touchstone for keeping the HR processes consistent with other changes to the organisation.

Having checked thoroughly, Huxley was over the moon that there wasn't in fact a great big wiggly snake in his dinghy ...

14 **Urging and celebrating**

In which Alex reviews the agency's sense of urgency

Having been with the agency for just over three months, Alex thought it time to review his own performance.

The agency's cash flow was as good as could have been expected. With Steve's help, Alex's original cost-cutting measures had started to work their way to the bottom line.

But even on the current course, the agency would still be breaching its covenants with its banks in two months' time. With little scope for further cost-saving, the only real hope lay in winning more business.

That was where the *Star Trek* plan would have to pay off. The industry teams that had been launched several months earlier were looking promising. And Alex had particular hopes regarding the team that was focusing on the Internet. In that area, the agency's reputation had received a strong boost from their successful pitch to Surf-Earn.com.

But Alex still wondered whether he should be doing more. As a prelude to reviewing his performance so far, Alex pulled from his briefcase a page of notes – the points he'd jotted down several months earlier, during his discussion with Michael.

He flicked back through his desk diary as he focused on two specific aspects of his leadership: whether he'd done enough to create a sense of urgency in the agency's staff, and whether he'd promoted enough celebration of the successes – however small – that they had so far achieved.

He awarded himself high marks on 'creating a sense of urgency', and for 'urging people on' more broadly. He felt he'd taken many steps both to impress on the staff that they had to deliver the agency's turnaround quickly, and also to urge, cajole, encourage and support them in their efforts.

● His first step had been to show his turnaround plan to the directors, as soon as he'd arrived as chief executive of the agency.

- As early as week 2, he'd brought the account directors and creatives face-to-face, eyeball-to-eyeball, with clients who had provided frank and irrefutable facts on how the agency needed to improve.
- He'd put in as many hours as had been needed to deliver his broader vision for the agency as early as week 3. And he'd made sure that the *whole* agency saw the videos of what the clients had said about them.
- He'd demonstrated by personal example the uncompromising efforts needed to win the Surf-Earn account.
- Regarding the Internet project, he'd been careful not to allow that apparently 'additional' initiative to languish – even though he'd had to cajole Doug into freeing up more of Len's time.
- And while his dismissal of Frank had been generally supported by the agency's staff, it had nevertheless impressed on them the urgent need to implement the *Star Trek* plans.

But Alex was not convinced that he'd promoted enough celebration.

He had of course been walking a delicate tightrope. Too little celebration risked the agency becoming demoralised – at the prospect of ever more work and ever less enjoyment. But he'd felt that too much celebration risked establishing a false sense of security, and thus decreasing the momentum.

Nevertheless, he now wondered whether he'd been too miserly with the celebration. They had certainly partied hard after the news of winning the Surf-Earn campaign, but Alex hadn't instigated many further festivities. He resolved to correct that imbalance, though only the winning of a major new client would justify full-scale revelling.

In the meantime, he planned to uncover smaller successes to celebrate. The effective collaboration between Sandra and Doug certainly warranted some form of recognition. Luke's eventual co-operation in extending the agency's intranet to embrace more of the traffic co-ordination function sprang to mind as a further example. After only a few minutes of concentration, Alex had a list of six further initiatives to celebrate.

Thinking back to 'urgency', Alex's only regret was that he hadn't visibly disposed of the art collection. That would have sent a truly powerful signal. But, faced with unanimous opposition to the disposal, he concluded that he'd taken the right action.

SUPPORTING VIM

Some of the leader's efforts focus specifically on creating vision, some focus on inspiration, and some on momentum. Other efforts act towards all three of these ends simultaneously. These latter efforts are: *a)* establishing and maintaining a sense of urgency while celebrating appropriately, *b)* personally demonstrating the values implied or stated in the vision, and *c)* corralling the organisation's attention throughout the life of the leader's mission.

URGING AND CELEBRATING

There is a continual risk that the leader's initiatives will under-perform, if the right people don't quite get around to providing sufficient input. Even committed agents of change too often apply the maxim of 'just do it … but later' when it comes to the extra work needed for the new initiative, or when critical resources need to be redirected.

Recognising this, effective leaders create a sense of urgency about new initiatives, and find novel ways to sustain them. This requires:

- **Early and frank discussion, radical debate and clear decisions by the leadership group.** This should yield agreed priorities, deadlines and responsibilities for action.

  Though this sounds straightforward, many leadership groups do make predictable errors: failing to marshal the relevant facts; remaining unconvinced by anecdotal though important evidence; or being unwilling to trust their intuition and hypotheses ('let's wait till we have more facts').
- **Subsequent personal action by the leader.** As illustrated on the opposite page, the effective leader uses the power of the organisation's informal 'grapevine' – refusing to rely purely on official programmes of 'mass communication' to urge the initiative on.

Throughout, the effective leader also fosters **celebration**.

MAINTAINING THE SENSE OF URGENCY

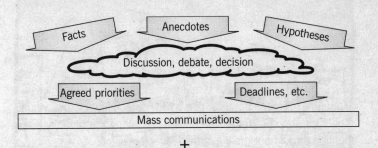

Mass communications

+

Leader's personal agenda	(Impact via 'the grapevine')
Personal meetings, with front line workers and project team members (often 'reaching round the formal hierarchy'), as well as with top managers and resource co-ordinators.	*'It must be important – he came all the way to see me.'*
Visible signals, from 'selling the company jet' to 'removing the chairs from board meetings, in order to focus discussions'.	*'He must mean it because …'*
Follow-ups, via scheduled reviews, as well as through ad hoc meetings with key personnel.	*'The way he acted in that review meeting means this must still be top priority.'*

EXERCISE

Review (or establish) your own agenda for sustaining the sense of urgency regarding an initiative you are leading.

As the crowd was turning ugly, Trapper Farrer figured something must have tipped them off ...

15 **Living the values**

In which Alex is the subject of 'corridor talk'

'This Alex guy – I'm still not so sure about him,' said Sandra, as she and Doug went out for lunch together – for the first time ever.

'How do you mean?' asked Doug.

'He's not exactly charismatic,' she replied.

'You mean he doesn't have flowing hair, a silver halo and a golden aura?'

'It's just that he seems pretty down-to-earth,' replied Sandra, 'no mystique, not a real charmer.'

'I know what you mean,' said Doug. 'But he does seem engaging enough. And he's certainly intelligent, courageous, and fair in how he deals with people.'

'I dunno,' countered Sandra. 'He keeps promoting this new culture – creativity and collaboration. But is he really creative himself?'

'Well he's certainly a team player – a collaborator. And, if you think about it, he has had some good ideas – like bringing in those clients to talk directly with your creatives and my account directors.'

'You call that a creative idea?' demanded Sandra.

Doug was about to respond by insulting Sandra's collection of so-called creative artwork. But he thought better of it – he was starting to enjoy talking with Sandra, and was already wondering whether to invite her out for dinner sometime.

□ □ □

Len and his junior colleague, Rachel, were having a quick sandwich lunch in the agency's canteen.

'So, what d'you reckon about our great leader?' asked Rachel.

'He's a pain in the ass,' muttered Len, recalling the five adland parties he'd been unable to attend. The combination of the IBM pitch and the Internet project was consuming all his waking hours.

'I think he's just what this agency needs,' asserted Rachel, who had never embraced the political correctness of agreeing with her immediate boss.

'And how come you're such an expert?' demanded Len.

'He really grilled me when I was interviewed for this job,' replied Rachel. 'It's the most thorough interview I've ever had.

'And what was so impressive about that?'

'We spent five minutes on the basics of my resumé,' she replied, 'but he spent most of the time probing on creativity and teamwork – not just abstract stuff – he wanted real examples. He even gave me that question about "why are manhole covers round?" You know, when he keeps spouting this new vision about creativity and teamwork, I'm sure he really means it. And from what I've seen of the agency so far, I think he's right.'

Len took a swig of Coke, glanced at Rachel, and wondered what impression he himself had made when interviewing this new recruit.

□ □ □

Luke and Terry were putting the finishing touches to a few new pages on the agency's intranet.

'D'you think we'll get this up and running on time?' asked Terry. 'My media guys are working flat out on other stuff – we can't count on much of their time if we need to make changes to these web pages.'

'We've got to meet the deadline,' replied Luke.

'How come?' asked Terry. 'Are you afraid of what Alex will do to you, if we're late?' He enjoyed ribbing the earnest Luke.

'Our new chief executive always delivers his contributions on time,' replied Luke as he clattered at his keyboard. 'So I don't think we can be late.'

□ □ □

Kelly was discussing arrangements for the agency's forthcoming summer party, with the other member of the organising committee – Sandra's secretary.

'I suppose there won't be much of a budget for this year's party,' said the creative director's secretary.

'That's right,' said Kelly. 'We've got a thousand pounds at most. That's less than twenty quid a head.'

'Has Alex had any creative ideas for the event?'

'I think he's expecting *us* to come up with the ideas,' Kelly pointed out.

'Doesn't surprise me.'

'Why do you say that?' asked Kelly, surprised.

'You know what Sandra says? She doesn't think Alex is creative enough for this agency,' confided Sandra's secretary.

'I thought his *Star Trek* video was a good idea,' said Kelly. 'And how about when he showed us those videos of the clients talking about the agency?'

'Sandra reckons they weren't Alex's ideas. She says Alex got some communications expert to dream up that stuff.'

Kelly looked at her in amazement. 'Well, you can tell Sandra that Alex did dream up those ideas for the presentation. I saw all the notes he was making, looking for something exciting and entertaining. If Sandra really does think Alex got advice from an expert, then she obviously does think Alex's ideas are creative, after all.'

LIVING THE VALUES

Being an excellent role model is the second way that the effective leader fortifies his process of creating vision, inspiration and momentum.

By direct observation, and through the virally infective power of the organisation's grapevine, people form their picture of the leader. Particularly at times of major change for the team (or for the organisation), the leader is also judged – and judged quickly.

The leader is examined by his followers for his general traits of leadership, such as courage, grace-under-pressure, and the other characteristics already referred to in appendix 2, page 146.

But mankind is an inveterate recogniser of patterns, and notices inconsistencies. So the organisation will also be deciding whether the leader lives up to the specific values and themes he is promoting within the organisation.

The leader's immediate team and contacts will notice how he behaves; they will tell others in the organisation; a story will develop about their leader. From apparently minuscule beginnings, the leader's legend is created – for better or for worse.

People not only judge the leader, however – many eventually emulate him too. The way in which the leader 'lives the values' has a massive effect on the organisation's culture.

The opposite page provides examples of how the effective leader will pass the tests that the organisation applies to him – and how those tests are sometimes failed by would-be leaders.

EXAMPLE OF LIVING THE VALUES

Potential for new 'theme' for the organisation	ACID TESTS FOR THE LEADER: Pass if the leader ...	Fail if the leader ...
Customer focus	Personally talks with customers to review levels of service.	Delegates customer research to the marketing department, and relies purely on their surveys.
Openness	Listens to, and acts on, personal feedback from potentially junior people.	Mounts programme to provide feedback to others, but does not himself visibly participate.
Creativity	Makes presentations in novel and engaging format.	Vetoes high-profile novel ideas – e.g., relating to company's intranet
Diversity	Seeks qualified members of relevant minority groups* to play senior roles.	Tolerates inappropriate behaviour by others towards members of minority groups.
Completed staff work	Over-delivers on results of own 'sleeves-rolled-up' work.	Fails to deliver because of major unforeseen crisis.
Personal touch	'It's amazing – he seems to know everyone in the company!' Amazes others with his uncanny ability to know everyone in the company.	'Where's he gone?! All I get is these e-mails!' Issues e-mails and memos, but is invisible to most people.
Collaboration	'I hear he's really working closely with that guy he used to loathe – I wonder what's happened?' Is seen to work with others – even with former 'rivals'.	'I couldn't believe how he badmouthed that other director.' Makes humorous but cynical remarks about others.

*'Minority groups' are not only racial groups but include functional groups such as 'salespeople', or types such as 'mavericks'

EXERCISE

Check whether you are visibly demonstrating the values you espouse. Ask your assistant – or someone else – what the grapevine is saying about you.

Just before the Battle of the Little Big Horn,
Custer promotes 'Ol' Phlegm' Magee to bugler …

16 Corralling attention

In which Alex checks his broadcast

Alex clicked on to the agency's intranet, and skimmed the home page. This was the first page that anyone in the agency met when entering the system, so Alex had been careful to control what appeared there.

Though the Internet team had been his most recent vehicle, Alex had used various means to corral the attention of the relevant audiences to his programme for change, during his sixteen weeks at DKNU.

Initially, he had grabbed the attention of his immediate leadership team by inviting face-to-face comments from clients, and by explaining his vision for the agency.

His next target audience had been those people who would be most affected by the *Star Trek* initiatives. Of the several visible and symbolic actions he'd taken to focus their minds, his justifiable firing of Frank – the Director of Planning – had been the most powerful.

But in the last few weeks, he'd wanted to corral the attention of the whole agency. It was important that everyone kept the *Star Trek* plan clearly in mind. That's why he had been so specific about the content of that first intranet page – which now highlighted the agency's most important indicators of performance. With his cost-cutting measures well under way, Alex's priority now was to increase revenues as fast as possible. So the home page was allotted exclusively to work that the agency had won recently. The number and size of the agency's wins (and losses) were the most important indicators of performance. These Key Performance Indicators (KPIs), as Alex frequently called them, were now on the system for all to see.

But teamwork and collaboration were also crucial, so the home page also had a relevant quote for the day. Today's thought was: Teamwork is vital – it gives you someone to blame! Alex did allow humour.

As Alex scanned the page, the results did look vaguely encouraging. '*Yup,*' he thought, '*I suppose everything's going as well as can be expected. Now we just need to land a really big client – and hope that none of our directors jumps ship to the competition ...*'

Satisfied with the intranet page, Alex suddenly wondered about the team that was meant to be exploring the agency's opportunities for gaining client work related to the Internet. He hadn't heard much from that team recently. He made a note to talk with Len and Doug about the project, because that team was another potentially powerful way to sustain the organisation's attention to collaboration, and to gaining new clients.

Alex looked up as Kelly entered his office.

'I wasn't sure whether to say anything,' Kelly began, 'but I was talking to Doug's secretary. She'd gone into his office to get some papers, and she saw something.'

Alex raised an eyebrow.

'Doug wasn't in his office,' she continued, 'but his diary was. And there was ... there was ... a meeting pencilled in – it's a meeting with Megaquest.com. I wasn't sure whether to tell you – perhaps you know about it anyway?'

'Megaquest.com?' repeated Alex. 'No – he hasn't mentioned anything about meeting with them. But why are you telling me this?'

'Yes ... uuh ... well,' Kelly resumed, 'I know someone at Cross & Rubicon.'

'Megaquest's current advertising agency?'

'Yes,' continued Kelly. 'We studied Media together at college. Anyway, she said their boss was planning to see Doug in a couple of days' time.'

'I see,' Alex replied. 'Thanks Kelly. You did the right thing by telling me.'

Alex's mind was racing. Doug's planning two secret meetings? One with Megaquest, which owns our new client Surf-Earn. And one with Cross & Rubicon, which is Megaquest's own ad agency! Alex paused.

Then the implications dawned on him, '*Doug must be planning to desert us, and join Cross & Rubicon. And he's probably planning to take the Surf-Earn account with him!*'

Alex set off in search of Doug. He couldn't find him in his office, though his secretary said he was in the building somewhere. Eventually Alex had him paged.

'We need to talk,' Alex started, as Doug arrived – looking agitated.

'Yes, we do,' agreed Doug.

Alex hesitated, wondering whether he should strike first.

'It's about Megaquest,' Doug blurted excitedly. 'I was on my way to tell you, but I stopped off in Sandra's office on the way.'

'Go on,' said Alex, warily.

'I've just had Megaquest's marketing director on the phone – he'll be in London next month. He's extremely impressed with our initial work for Surf-Earn. But Megaquest.com is planning a global campaign of its own – and he wants to meet us, to talk about it. I tried to call you – but you and Kelly were both on the phone. I've pencilled in a meeting – I said I'd get back to them, once I'd checked with you and Sandra.'

Alex's face crumpled into a weird expression, as he simultaneously let out a sigh of relief while inhaling in amazement. '*Perhaps this isn't a desertion, after all*,' he thought, '*but what about that meeting Doug's planning with Cross & Rubicon?*'

'Are you feeling OK?' asked Doug.

'Uuh … well, I was just wondering about Cross & Rubicon,' probed Alex. 'I thought they were entrenched there?'

'Don't worry about them,' said Doug. 'I'm having a clandestine meeting with someone I know there. I'll get the inside scoop before we meet with Megaquest.com.'

CORRALLING ATTENTION

The effective leader is adept at grabbing attention for his proposals and initiatives. He 'stays on the balcony'.

He has the uncanny knack of knowing which people need to provide support during successive stages of the organisation's programmes for change. Early in these programmes, the effective leader targets individuals and teams that can help him set direction. Then he focuses on those people who can turn a programme's vision into reality. Finally, he aims for the attention of most – or all – of the organisation.

Four powerful tools for grabbing attention are:

1 **A clearly articulated vision,** conveyed with a sense of urgency (as set out in earlier chapters).
2 **High-profile actions, which symbolise the ways the organisation is to work.** Examples range from 'selling the company jet' (to highlight financial prudence), through to 'promoting mavericks' (to emphasise the organisation's need for creativity or radical thinking).
3 **Active management of the 'grapevine'.** Communications rarely flow along the lines suggested by the official organisation chart. The effective leader is therefore careful to feed the 'grapevine' with appropriate information.
4 **The choice of 'Key Indicators of Performance'.** Eventually, managers and operational staff will be monitoring the organisation's renewed progress. The effective leader checks that the 'closely-watched numbers' are germane to the changes he has tried to bring about in the organisation. For example, if the mission is to have the organisation sell products that are more profitable, he may require management reports to highlight each salesperson's financial contribution rather than merely their turnover.

The facing page summarises how the leader gears his communications to specific audiences, in line with his overall programme for change.

PERVASIVE COMMUNICATION

During the three main phases of the change programme, the effective leader corrals the attention of various audiences in turn, using specific tools to communicate.

Overall programme:

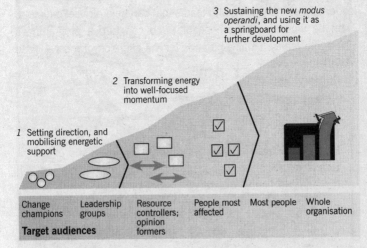

3 Sustaining the new *modus operandi*, and using it as a springboard for further development

2 Transforming energy into well-focused momentum

1 Setting direction, and mobilising energetic support

| Change champions | Leadership groups | Resource controllers; opinion formers | People most affected | Most people | Whole organisation |

Target audiences

Tools to target communications:

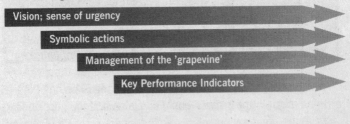

Vision; sense of urgency

Symbolic actions

Management of the 'grapevine'

Key Performance Indicators

EXERCISE

For an initiative you are leading, assess whether you are focusing on the correct audiences – and whether you are retaining their attention.

Barnshaw had the neatest trench on the Front,
but it didn't win him any medals.

17 **Leading or managing?**

In which Alex becomes a leader-breeder

During the next few days, Alex had spent long hours in the office. Caffeine and adrenalin sustained him as he threw himself into preparing for the meeting with Megaquest.com. Megaquest could yet become the agency's saviour.

But Alex did find time to talk to Len about the flagging Internet team that Len was supposed to be leading. Alex waded through the discarded paraphernalia of previous advertising campaigns that crammed Len's office, and sat down opposite him.

'Do you have a couple of minutes?' asked Alex. 'We need to talk about the Internet project.'

'Sure – I know how important that project is,' said Len, preparing his defences. 'To be honest, I've had real difficulty getting enough input from the others. We're all too busy on other things … it's certainly the toughest project I've ever managed …'

'The toughest project you've managed, or the toughest you've led?' probed Alex. 'I mean … how do you see your role?'

Len searched for a politically correct answer, but ended up focusing on the tangible: his workplan. 'I see my role as making sure that we all know what we're meant to contribute – the end products we've all agreed on, and the deadlines.' Len excavated through the papers on his desk, and proudly produced his master workplan.

Alex had seen the workplan during previous reviews, but he now saw it in a slightly different light. In a way, he thought it resembled the type of plan with which he himself had arrived at the agency four months earlier. 'Your plan looks very professional,' said Alex. 'But it hasn't had much impact yet. How can I help you, as you lead this project: on the technical side of the market research? Or on your role as leader? Or on some other aspect of the project?'

'Thanks for your offer,' replied Len, 'but I think I can manage OK.'

'I'm sure you can *manage* OK,' replied Alex. 'But I see you as a future leader in this agency – not just a manager – and I'd like to offer you a couple of tips.'

Len was not about to refuse the offer. He sat taller, flattered that the chief executive had bothered to think about him in this way.

'From what I've seen,' started Alex, 'your strengths as a manager are distracting you from some of the things you need to do as a leader.'

'I've noticed – on other projects – that you're good at sustaining momentum,' continued Alex. 'That's something which both managers and leaders need to do. But I suspect you need to do more to inspire your team members – and to help them have a vision of their success, not merely a workplan. That's the difference between being a leader and being a manager. I'll send you a few pages on the subject.'*

'I'm not quite following you,' admitted Len.

'OK – how many times have you met with your four team members?' asked Alex.

'We've had two team meetings, and two progress reviews with the management committee.'

'And how often have you met with the team members individually – to kick around ideas, or to see if there are problems?' continued Alex.

'I guess I haven't actually met with any of them individually,' replied Len. 'We normally just e-mail each other.'

'Why not try getting more personal with your team-mates,' suggested Alex. '"Management by e-mail" might work, but "leadership by e-mail" won't.'

'But doesn't that take more time?' asked Len. 'E-mails are much more efficient.'

'Perhaps in the short term,' conceded Alex, 'but leaders focus on effectiveness, not just on efficiency. And another thing – if the people on your team merely see you whipping up a quick workplan, and dispatching a few e-mails, then they're hardly going to

---

*See page 102.

be inspired to put much of their own time and effort into the project.'

'I see what you're saying,' Len replied, nodding yet unconvinced.

'At the risk of labouring the point,' Alex persevered, 'take this discussion as an example. I think you'll act differently as a result of my talking to you personally than if I'd merely sent you an e-mail.'

Now Len understood.

'So try to get personal,' continued Alex. 'Remember that inventories can be managed, but people need to be led. And one last point: ask yourself: "What is the biggest risk I'm taking on this project?" I'm not saying you should aim for unnecessary risk. But if it doesn't feel at least a bit risky then the project probably won't truly excite your team members. And you're probably not going to come up with radical ideas. Don't forget,' he added, 'we're counting on you to be radical. After all, we're trying to "explore new lands, and to boldly go" especially with this Internet project.'

□ □ □

After his brief discussion with Len on leading and managing, Alex glanced at his watch and raced back to his office, realising that he was meant to be at a meeting on the other side of town. This was one of several meetings he'd set up – with people who could help him in preparing for the forthcoming meeting with Megaquest.com.

But dipping into his diary, he realised that he'd overlooked a conflicting meeting with the bankers. He'd been sure that meeting had been set for the following day. As he reached for the phone to sort out the problem, Kelly appeared at his office door.

'I've just had a call from *Campaign Weekly*,' she said. 'They're about to run a story on the agency. The reporter said it won't be favourable – but he asked if you want to comment. You've got half an hour before they put the story to bed.'

Alex had not had a cigarette for twelve months, but now he felt that he couldn't continue on adrenalin and caffeine alone …

LEADING AND MANAGING

Leading is fundamentally different from managing. Put briefly:

- The effective leader seeks out situations where change is needed. He 'does the right thing', and operates using personal influence. He is stronger on **'vision'**, and often on **'inspiration'** too.
- The efficient manager makes change happen. He 'does things right' and relies more on positional influence. **'Momentum'** is his strong suit, and ideally (but alas less frequently) he can also **'inspire'**.

All organisations need managers as well as leaders. Without strong managers, the organisation risks descending into chaos.

But without effective leaders, the organisation becomes lethargic and fails to evolve. Unfortunately, all but the best organisations have less leadership talent than they need (and less than they believe they have). All too often, executives are assumed to be leaders by virtue of having the right title or position. And if those people manage where they ought to be leading, the results will be mediocre at best.

In most organisations, therefore, an important task of true leaders is to breed other leaders. Only by doing so can the organisation expect to survive – let alone thrive. Though training courses may help to breed leaders, the best organisations know this growth of talent can only come through relevant experiences.

This involves either a 'radical' experience – where the would-be leader is seconded to a situation in which he has both the 'elbow room' and the obligation to lead; or a 'role-modelling' experience – in which the would-be leader is able to learn from a relevant mentor.

□ □ □

The effective leader is also careful not to lapse back into 'managing', as we shall see in the next chapter.

LEADERSHIP CONTRASTED WITH MANAGEMENT

Leaders differ from managers in the way they develop a 'vision', as indicated below. They also differ in their approach to inspiration and momentum, as indicated in appendix 8, page 156.

Manager	Leader
Does things right	Does the right thing
Focuses on the present, the short term and the bottom line	Focuses on the future, the long term and the horizon
Seeks order	Relishes change
Contains risks	Takes risks
Appeals more to reason than to emotion	Appeals to both emotion and reason

Less leadership necessary when organisational unit is:

- Smaller department, *and*
- Already operating at best practice, *and*
- Not facing substantial external threats

More leadership required when organisational unit is:

- Larger company, *or*
- Presented with major development opportunities, *or*
- Facing substantial external threats

EXERCISE

Hone your own skills in leadership by coaching a manager to become a leader.

ATILLA THE NUN

*As leadership types went, Attila the Nun wasn't perfect –
but at least conversions were up 61%.*

18 **Roles and delegation**

In which Alex starts to behave strangely

'It smells like you've had a cigarette,' said Sarah a few days later, as Alex came home from the office. He was just in time for the dinner to which they'd invited Michael.

'Maybe one, or two,' admitted Alex cautiously. He glanced down the hall and into the living room, and could see that Michael had already arrived.

Though Michael was a good friend, and had been immensely supportive throughout Alex's career, Alex would have preferred to spend the evening without him. There was too much work still to do – and Alex had brought some of it home with him.

But the table was set, and the food was about to burn. Alex resigned himself to working after dinner, and late into the night.

'So tell me about the agency,' said Michael. 'I haven't heard from you in the last month. I did read about you in *Campaign Weekly*, of course. I thought the article was pretty good, under the circumstances.'

'It would have been a lousy article if I hadn't spent an hour on the phone with the journalist,' replied Alex.

The conversation continued – about the company in which Alex and Michael had formerly worked together, about friends they had in common, but mainly about the agency.

Sarah and Michael both cracked jokes, but Alex failed to understand the punch-lines. He seemed preoccupied, and only came to life when the phone rang with a call from one of the agency's account directors.

As Alex returned to the table, he could see that Sarah and Michael had been discussing him.

'You've talked a lot about the agency,' said Michael. 'But what about your own role? You seem busier than I've ever seen you before.'

'Turning around a company is a busy job,' snapped Alex.

Sarah and Michael exchanged glances at Alex's brusqueness.

'Are you feeling OK?' asked Michael. 'We don't want you ending up like that chap Rob.'

Rob had been Alex's predecessor as chief executive of the agency. Rob had indeed predeceased Alex – caught in the grip of a fatal coronary.

'Don't worry about me – I'll be fine,' replied Alex. 'It's just that I'm under a lot of pressure. I've got the whole change programme to run. Then there's all the cost-cutting initiatives – I've got to make sure we haven't missed any opportunities. There are job descriptions which need to be redone – we managed without the new versions for a while, but now we really need them.

'Then there are the banks to be kept happy, and some legal problems to do with someone I had to fire. There's only one piece of good news: we've had the chance to make a pitch to a company called Megaquest.com. If I win that, then I think things will get easier for a while ...'

He paused in mid flow as Michael raised his hand. 'Yes?' barked Alex.

'What did you mean when you said: "If *I* win that pitch?"' asked Michael, not intimidated.

Alex looked at him as if his friend had gone mad.

'Why on earth do *you* need to lead that pitch?' asked Michael.

'Look, Michael – I'm the Chief Executive, and Megaquest is potentially the biggest client in the history of the agency. Need I say more?'

'Yes,' replied Michael firmly. 'Tell me why you are getting so involved in all the preparations for that pitch – all those meetings with people outside the agency. Haven't you got any account directors to do that? I hope you've got some good account directors – because *you* are meant to be running an advertising agency!'

'It's important for my credibility,' answered Alex.

'But you personally won that pitch to Surf-Earn,' said Sarah. 'You told me a few months ago that you'd really earned your spurs on that pitch. Why can't you delegate most of the work on this one? I know you'll need to be present at the meeting with Megaquest.com – but you don't have to do all the work for it!'

Despite his crazed approach to life in the past few weeks, Alex was still capable of rational thought. 'Perhaps I have got too involved,' he conceded. 'But I had to. None of the account directors could do these preparations as well as I can.'

The phone rang again, and Sarah went into the hall to answer it. 'That was Rob ...' she said, looking straight at Alex.

'Rob?' Alex repeated. He gulped. 'It can't be. Rob's dead!'

'Not *that* Rob,' she continued, turning to Michael. 'Someone called Rob Moreno – about the mini-cab you'd ordered? He went to the wrong address. The cab will be here in a few minutes.'

Shocked that the other Rob might have come back from the grave to haunt him, Alex finally started to think about his own role.

'If you're a leader who has already achieved some success,' said Michael, 'the biggest mistake you can make is to invest your time in things that are most important to your organisation.' The statement surprised both Alex and Sarah.

'You have to ask yourself two questions, not just one: what's important for the organisation? And – in addition – where am I uniquely qualified to add value? Many leaders only ask the first question. That's a big mistake.'

Michael got up to retrieve his coat. 'If you're overworked, it's either because you're intrinsically unwilling to delegate, or because you haven't thought about it enough.

'There are times when you should lead, times to be a chairman, times to be a coach, or an enforcer or a spokesman. But only get drawn into the details of things which you are uniquely qualified to address.'

SIX ROLES TO PLAY

The effective leader is able to play a variety of roles. It is as if he has a pack of cards, each of which corresponds to a role – and each of which he is able to play at the appropriate time. These roles are:

1 **Leader** – initiating new missions and creating vision, inspiration and momentum in other people.
2 **Chairman** – setting the agenda for discussions; encouraging thorough debate; gaining broad agreement to conclusions if possible; casting his deciding vote if necessary.
3 **Spokesman** – representing the organisation to external constituencies and stakeholders.
4 **Coach** – identifying when others are not achieving their full potential; helping to develop their skill or will.
5 **Enforcer/Manager** – reviewing progress; specifying corrective action, or taking it.
6 **Participant** – occasionally (when uniquely qualified) contributing to a project that is being led by someone else, e.g., serving major clients or customers.

The effective leader clearly spends the majority of his time on the first of these roles. In addition, he is explicit with himself and with other people when he plays the less usual roles – to avoid confusing people about his intentions, about his personal agenda, or about the responsibilities of others.

But the effective leader knows that he could potentially get drawn into the details of every issue that the organisation faces. He therefore also delegates aggressively – a tool for which is suggested on the next page.

DECIDING HOW INVOLVED TO BECOME

The effective leader avoids involving himself in everything. He focuses on issues which are both *1)* important to the organisation, and also *2)* where he can add particular value (top right-hand box).

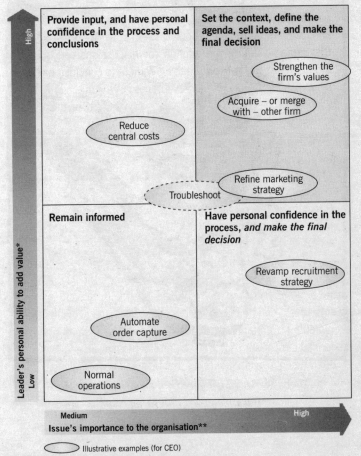

Illustrative examples (for CEO)

*Criteria: unique perspective, signalling role as figurehead, personal skills, driver of objectives for high performance, relative skills of other managers.
** Criteria: impact on external reputation, impact on culture, impact on institutional skills, impact on bottom line.

Major Searles would have been the first to agree that this wasn't a good time to 'go blank'.

19 Phasing and timing

In which Alex rings some changes

In the few days after his dinner conversation with Michael, Alex resolved to free up more of his time, by delegating more effectively to his directors.

He met with Doug, officially 'handing over' the preparations for the Megaquest.com pitch exclusively to him and his account directors. Not only had that freed up some of Alex's time – it had also strengthened his relationship with Doug. Doug had apparently thought Alex hadn't trusted him to do the work. He had been about to tackle Alex on the subject, and was relieved that Alex had initiated the discussion.

The following Monday, Alex was chairing the weekly management meeting. They started – as usual – by reviewing the progress of the 'housekeeping' plan that had focused on reducing costs. Under Steve's leadership, those initiatives were now almost complete. But they had saved fewer costs than planned. The rebates from the over-funded pension plan were smaller than had been expected, as had been the savings on 'unbilled production costs' – costs which the creatives had deigned to start controlling.

Despite the positive impact of Alex's visionary *Star Trek* initiatives, however, the directors knew the agency would not survive for more than a few weeks unless their cash position improved substantially.

'What's this exceptional credit of three hundred thousand pounds?' asked Luke, as they turned to review the agency's finances.

'This time it can't be a rebate on TV airtime that we've bought,' said Terry. 'I've had my media guys go through our numbers with a fine toothcomb.'

'It's a tax credit,' said Steve, glancing at Alex. 'I managed to recoup it because we had those cocktail ads shot in Bermuda.'

'Come on,' said Luke. 'We've had almost a million pounds of

exceptional credits over the past couple of months. I'm not complaining about the cash injections ... but how can we tell where we stand when these unexpected items are so large?'

'This really is the last of those credits,' Alex intervened. 'We can't rely on any more of them. We'll just have to hope that next week's meeting with Megaquest.com goes well. Now, let's move on.'

'I'd like us to discuss the Internet project,' said Sandra. 'Doug's shown me the team's latest work – and it looks pretty convincing. I think it's time we publicised it to potential clients.'

'I agree,' said Alex. 'I've always thought we could become the top UK agency in this field. All we need is to find the right ways to present our research. We should definitely aim for a write-up in the *FT*, as well as approaching target clients to discuss our findings ...' Alex went on to set out his vision of how to make best use of the Internet team's research.

But then he paused. He paused for two reasons. Firstly, he realised that he was again involving himself too much in detailed planning. He knew his role was to chair the meeting – not to begin solving the problem.

And secondly, he noticed that he was starting with a vision. It was a rough sketch of what needed to happen – in the same way as he'd started to sketch out his *Star Trek* plans, nearly five months earlier.

He suddenly realised that 'starting with a vision, then creating inspiration and momentum' had become a habit. Often that habit was appropriate. But he now realised that it was sometimes better for the apparent leader to provide virtually none of his own input into creating the vision. As long as the relevant team members had roughly the same goal in mind, it was often better for the team to come up with a vision by themselves. That way, they would probably be more creative. And they would certainly be more convinced by the eventual vision and plans, once they had done their work. In other words, in favourable circumstances the leader could start with inspiration – and then contribute a bit of his own vision later, if necessary.

There were even times, he realised, when the leader had to start with momentum – some tangible actions prior to the stages of creating vision and inspiration. He thought back to his directors' initial cynicism when he'd suggested the new collaborative approach to pitching. In the end, he'd started by 'just doing it'. He'd led the pitch to Surf-Earn as a demonstration of how the new approach could work in practice. Only after the success of that pitch had there been the basis for shaping the vision and creating the inspiration – leading eventually to broader teamwork.

'I'm sorry,' said Alex, refocusing on the meeting. 'Sandra – why don't you tell us how you'd like us to promote this Internet research. After that, I suggest we discuss any last-minute issues regarding next week's meeting with Megaquest.com.'

PHASING AND TIMING

Phasing. When mounting an initiative, the effective leader knows he cannot always use the vision-inspiration-momentum techniques in that order.

For example, he may realise that the vision for change should be seen to emerge from some person other than himself, or from some group. In either case, he may first need to inspire the relevant individuals to work together – even before airing his own vision for the organisation.

Thus, the effective leader is always alert to the need for re-ordering the types of action set out in earlier chapters of this book, or for the need to take some of them in parallel.

Timing. The effective leader marshals his energy prudently – knowing that the organisation's demands on him are potentially infinite.

- Some projects demand an early burst of his input, but require less of it later – so he consciously 'reins back' after his initial involvement. This is typically the case when there is:
  - Agreement to the need for change.
  - Agreement to the direction of change.
  - An existing cadre of influential proponents, and an absence of powerful resisters.
  - An action-oriented culture in which people are used to meeting dead lines.
- When these conditions are not met, he identifies when to time his input for maximum effect.

  For example, he recognises situations in which people need time to digest ideas. His early steps in these cases may be merely to plant the seeds of the vision. While those seeds germinate, the leader will invest his time elsewhere.

INVESTING EFFORT

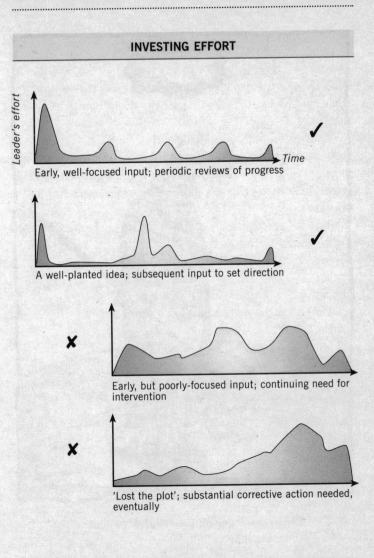

Early, well-focused input; periodic reviews of progress

A well-planted idea; subsequent input to set direction

Early, but poorly-focused input; continuing need for intervention

'Lost the plot'; substantial corrective action needed, eventually

EXERCISE

Draw the profile of how you plan to invest your energy in the 3–4 projects of greatest importance to you. Establish whether you can use different 'timing' to increase the effectiveness of your input.

There's power and then there's absolute power ...

20 Power and influence

In which Alex sees that 'power' is not a dirty word

For the first time in months, Alex had time to review his own e-mails. No longer did Kelly have to print them all out, for him to work on at home. He worked his way down the list of messages, eventually clicking on one from Michael.

'Thanks for dinner last week,' it read. 'Hope you now have time to skim this. If you do have the time, it means you're probably ready to visit http://www.leadership-skills.org.uk power.'

Clicking on the hyperlink, Alex found the following article:

EXCERPT

POWER: OBSERVATIONS AND TECHNIQUES FOR LEADERS

Even for people who intend to exercise it responsibly, the notion of power carries vaguely unsavoury undertones. Few people in any democracy would relish being called Machiavellian. 'Power' is a word that makes us edgy.

But the leader can be effective only if he deals in power or in its close relative: influence. For the leader will not always succeed by persuading people – or even by directing them.

This note briefly examines the nature of power in the modem organisation, and suggests ways in which the leader can acquire and use it.

The nature of power

We shall start with a definition of power. Or rather, we shall start with several definitions – for 'power' is an elusive term on which experts rarely agree precisely.

- According to Pfeffer, power is 'the potential ability to influence behaviour, to change the course of events, to overcome resistance, and to get people to do things they would not otherwise do' (*Managing with Power*).
- According to Gardner, power is 'the capacity to ensure the outcomes one wishes, and to prevent those one does not wish' (*On Leadership*).
- According to Kotter: 'Successful managers use the power they develop in their relationships, along with persuasion, to influence people on whom they are dependent to behave in ways that make it possible for the managers to get their jobs done' (*John P. Kotter on What Leaders Really Do*).

But despite their differences in emphasis, most experts do agree on one thing: there are few situations nowadays in which anyone (including the chief executive) possesses anything that comes even close to being absolute power.

The modern leader is hedged by constraints which his fore-bears did not know: workers' rights, anti-competition laws, efficient capital markets, and (perhaps most crucially) the ever-increasing mobility of labour.

Thus, the modern leader is actually highly dependent on other people, virtually all of the time. Robert Browning put this point succinctly: 'It is a strange desire to seek power and to lose liberty.' And, though talking of mankind in general, Alexander Pope echoed the sentiment: 'Great Lord of all things, yet a prey to all.'

And although corporate executives do sometimes lock horns (each under the false presumption that they do have absolute power), the leader who regularly gores others to death is eventually ejected from the herd.

It is therefore important to recognise that power is really *influence*, and to acknowledge that influence involves relationships of reciprocity with (or dependence on) the leader. So, in acquiring and using power the effective leader knows:

1 What he wants to happen.
2 Which people can make those things happen.
3 What 'currencies' he has, to trade with those people.

Often those 'currencies' are remuneration, prestige, working conditions and power itself. Sometimes the 'currencies' are variants of the previous list, such as privileged access to experience or education.

But what really matters is the *perception* that the leader can grant these things. As a result, the effective leader deals with three aspects of power, as discussed below: acquiring it, deploying it responsibly, and managing perceptions. To some extent these facets are related. For example, by exercising power, the leader builds the perception that he is indeed powerful.

Acquiring power
The most important outcomes that the leader needs (or merely wants) to influence obviously depend on the nature of the leader's organisation. In a bank, for example, the crucial outcomes usually

involve the way that money is raised or invested. In a law firm, those outcomes are often the way that clients are served, and the way that people are staffed and elected to partnership.

Whatever the organisation, however, the effective leader tends to use the following techniques to increase his power:

1 **Obtaining critical resources and staying personally involved in decisions to invest them.** For example, the person who aspires to power within a bank might ensure he is a member of the most influential investment committees. The lawyer might try to 'own' the largest client, or chair the committee that elects new partners.

2 **Obtaining agreement to broad formal authority for him- or herself.** The banker will acquire large lending rights. The lawyer will acquire important signatory authorities.

3 **Building alliances with other powerful people or groups – both inside and outside the organisation or team.** The banker will build strong personal relationships with people who can provide substantial funds to the bank, or who can bring large opportunities for investment. The lawyer will chair professional forums.

4 **Recognising that 'information is power', and establishing multiple networks of communication.** The effective leader acquires his information through access to reports, through informal contacts, and sometimes through trading it with other people.

5 **Increasing the degree to which others depend on him, or to which they are in his debt.** This dependence is often created by the leader's perceived ability to take the steps listed above. Sometimes the leader creates this dependence through less obvious means – e.g., through coaching or counselling others. Occasionally, dependence derives from a leader's unique technical expertise.

6 **Honing his or her personal skills** of eloquence, sensitivity, forcefulness and technical competence.

However, each organisation has its own cultural norms for both acquiring power, and for deploying it. The effective leader is sensitive to the bounds of 'legitimate' behaviour. He breaches them (ideally) only when trying to effect a radical positive change in the organisation's way of working.

Deploying power

Adept dealers in power know precisely 'how far they can go' – and then go to that extreme if necessary.

Only with practice can people accurately estimate their potential limits for exercising power, or meet them. Inexperienced leaders often assume that their emperor's clothing is more threadbare (or more glittering) than it truly is. They may also 'pull their punches' through lack of courage – or conversely 'go a bridge too far'.

With more or less of this insight into themselves, effective leaders take three types of action when using power and influence to achieve their goals:

1. **Using the full gamut of interpersonal skills.** The effective leader is able (in order of increasing coercion) to: comment, model, teach, appeal, persuade, negotiate and/or demand. The more the leader is able to use these styles appropriately, the greater is his perceived power.

2. **Making tactical moves.** Though the range of potential tactics is large, the ones that effective leaders employ most frequently are as follows:

   - Taking symbolic actions – to confer visible authority on proponents of the proposed changes, or to neutralise resisters of change, or to vest strategic themes with the leader's seal of approval.
   - Establishing temporary task forces or working groups – to work around pockets of resistance.
   - Revealing information selectively – either to influence decisions, or as a 'currency' in forging alliances.
   - Timing initiatives propitiously: advancing the timing of decisions or actions that need to take effect while the leader still has 'the upper hand'; delaying initiatives until the leader

is prepared or ready; setting deadlines, when the leader wants explicit action; avoiding the imposition of deadlines, when the leader wants to avert action.

3 **Making structural changes.** Under this heading, the leader may change reporting lines; amend levels of authority (e.g., spending limits); establish new governance bodies (to focus the organisation's attention, as well as to get things done), or change reporting systems (so that people pay attention to the things that the leader considers most important).

Experienced leaders often use several of these techniques together. And at critical moments, such combinations can be truly potent.

Kotter, for example, tells the story of a manager charged with turning around the failing division of a corporation. This manager gave just two hours' notice of his arrival, arrived with six assistants, then immediately called a meeting of all 40 top managers. At this meeting he outlined his assessment of the situation, his commitment to turn things around, and the basic direction he wanted things to move in.

The new boss then fired the four top managers in the room and gave them two hours to leave the building; he said he would dedicate himself to sabotaging the career of anyone who tried to block his efforts to save the division; and ended the 60-minute meeting by announcing that his assistants would be setting up appointments for him to meet the managers individually, starting at 7:00 the next morning. People co-operated with him.

Managing perceptions
The leader publicises his power primarily by deploying it. But he also 'manages his reputation' (ensuring that the corporate mythology includes appropriate stories of his own prowess); and he ensures that his technical performance (e.g., in selling or finance) is recognised.

But he also follows Kipling's advice not to 'look too smart, nor talk too wise', and Roosevelt's advice to talk softly (while carrying a big stick).

□ □ □

Leaders do use all of these techniques for acquiring power, and deploying it. And the techniques do work in the appropriate situations. But they can also backfire disastrously if used in amateurish ways.

For in the long term, few contrived applications of these techniques can match the power of irrefutable facts or the authority of irresistible ideas.

□ □ □

Alex clicked the web-page closed. He resolved to take stock of his own sources and uses of power.

But that task would have to wait for a few days. Of top priority now was the meeting with Vic McGovern and his colleagues at Megaquest.com, scheduled for the following Monday.

No one had mentioned it, but Ralph was pretty certain that even the Beagle had spotted his fake eyeball ...

21 **Culture**

In which Alex, Doug and Sandra go in to battle

The following Monday, Alex, Doug and Sandra were clambering out of a taxi, and entering the offices of Megaquest.com. They were all nervous, but they wore well-practised smiles of confidence.

Vic McGovern was Megaquest's International Marketing Director. It was he who would decide which agency to engage. During the course of several phone calls, Kelly had fortunately struck up a good relationship with Vic's secretary. She'd discovered that Megaquest was considering three other agencies, but none of them had made their pitches yet. That disappointed Alex, who preferred to go last in these 'beauty parades'. Going last made it easier to address any issues that the competing agencies might not have covered, and made it more likely that the potential client would remember you.

As the three from DKNU checked in at reception, they were all scanning the environment for clues regarding Megaquest's culture. They continued to scan as they met Vic's secretary, followed her to the elevator, and entered the glass-walled conference room. But they couldn't immediately spot any cultural clues to use in positioning their imminent presentation.

Vic arrived a few minutes later, with three colleagues. They introduced themselves, confirmed what they wanted to find out from the presentation, and handed the floor to Alex. Alex made a few remarks, but the most important part of the meeting was going to be led by Doug and Sandra.

And that was where they would be playing the first trump card. For there was a time-honoured tradition that all agencies observed: the account director presented the market research on which the agency had developed some initial advertising ideas – and the creative director presented those ideas to the client. The whole industry worked that way.

But Alex had suggested they break with that tradition. It would be Sandra who would run through the market research, then Doug would present their initial creative ideas. Alex was betting that the proof of collaboration would impress Vic.

Alex watched for Vic's reaction as Sandra started her spiel. He saw Vic lean forward and check her title from the business card she'd handed him earlier. He saw Vic sit back with a quizzical expression. Then saw the slight smile of understanding, as Vic turned towards him.

'*So far, so good*,' thought Alex.

Several hours later, with Doug and Sandra finished, Alex added a few concluding remarks. But the most difficult part of the pitch was now to come – the question and answer session. Alex knew this was where they would be most exposed, and he prayed that they'd anticipated the questions well enough.

' I'll be blunt,' Vic started. 'I'm expecting the other three agencies to have the same market research data to show, the same spiel about teamwork with their clients and within the agency, and similar lists of creative credentials. What's so special about *your* way of working?'

Alex and his colleagues had, of course, rehearsed for this question. But they all knew that Vic would be paying more attention to whether the people from DKNU really believed what they were saying, than to the specific words they used.

Vic peered at Alex, awaiting his answer.

So Vic was surprised when the reply came from DKNU's Creative Director. Vic knew that creatives normally couldn't care less about the broader management practices of their agencies. And he knew that most agencies wouldn't even risk letting the client see the creative director!

Sandra started to talk about DKNU's approach to teamwork, but both she and Vic knew that their first exchanges were mere pleasantries.

Vic was going to cross-examine Sandra until she'd revealed everything about how the agency really worked. Alex crossed his fingers, as Vic showed signs of being a professional interrogator.

□ □ □

Later, in the taxi back to the office, Alex congratulated Doug and Sandra on their double-act. 'That must have taken quite some rehearsing,' he added.

'Thanks,' replied Doug. 'But I really liked that line of yours at the end, Alex. I suppose it wasn't difficult to find out that Vic had been in advertising before he jumped into marketing – the reverse of our own career jumps.

'But I liked the way you put it: "You're a poacher turned game-keeper, and we are gamekeepers turned poachers, so that either makes us incompatible, or it makes us highly complementary." That was a great line.'

'Yes,' agreed Sandra. 'But if we win this pitch, it will be because we could really demonstrate the culture of teamwork and creativ-ity and industry expertise that we've created over the last six months. And do you know what? I'm sure the other agencies can't be as convincing as we were.'

'We'll find out soon enough,' observed Alex.

SHAPING THE CULTURE

What is an organisation's 'culture'? It is probably best described as 'the way we do things around here'. The culture is reflected in the set of behaviours that are considered normal by the members of the team or corporation, including the way that people communicate with each other and with the outside world. Of course, these behaviours are driven ultimately by individuals' mental models of the organisation, and creeds, as indicated on the opposite page.

A strong and positive culture is of immense value to the organisation. It allows people to communicate quickly (in the organisation's own shorthand), it allows people to 'do things right' (without having to consult detailed rulebooks), and it reduces the need for people to 'reinvent wheels'.

Obviously, a culture cannot be moulded overnight. But the effective leader daily tries to add a potent drop to the ocean that is the organisation's culture.

This he does in three main ways:

1   Addressing the organisation's habits, rituals and ceremonies directly. He inaugurates some and dissolves others – to create consistency with the organisation's vision, strategy, required skills, and system of beliefs.
2   Addressing these behaviours indirectly, using the approaches already mentioned in *Ways to Reinforce the Communication of the Change Program* (appendix 6, page 153).
3   Acting as a highly visible role-model of the required behaviours, as previously set out in *Living the Values* (chapter 15, page 87).

In aggregate, these initiatives demand much of the leader – but are essential if his organisation is to thrive in the long term.

ASPECTS OF CULTURE

Visible aspects of culture are based on mental models, and ultimately on creeds.

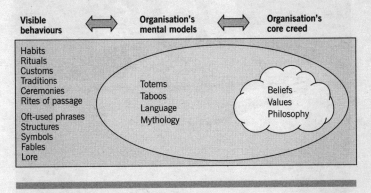

Example of using 'rites of passage'

An international consumer products company had operations around the globe. The managers clearly needed to co-ordinate their marketing and production strategies, but managers from different regions rarely knew each other well.

Over several years, the company gradually established its own school of brand management – in which each course had a highly international mix of participants. It became a 'rite of passage' because attendance at the school became a prerequisite for being promoted (or hired) to the position of manager.

It succeeded in creating the required 'organisational glue' because the courses lasted long enough (and had sufficient 'social' time) for people to 'bond' with each other – and to embrace the company's 'creed'.

EXERCISE

Review the behaviours of a team or organisation you are leading (or in which you are participating). Identify one bad habit that needs to be broken – or a positive one that needs to be developed. Plan how you will make that change.

Little did Snowy know, as he barked I-C-E-B-E-R-G-! in Morse code, that Hornblower's hearing aid had missed its last service …

22 **The VIM of self-leadership**

In which Alex's future is decided

Several days later, Alex arrived at work unnecessarily early. Megaquest.com would be announcing its choice of agency for its global campaign. But that wasn't likely to be before nine a.m. New York time. That meant waiting until at least two o'clock in London.

Alex spent most of the morning, and most of his sandwich lunch, with Steve – checking that the cost-saving parts of his turn-around plan were producing results. Yes, the car fleet had been sold to the bank and leased back. Yes, they'd completed the pro-gramme of switching to less expensive suppliers of everything from plane tickets to photocopy paper. Yes, they'd received the final payment from the over-funded pension contributions.

'We're just keeping our heads above water,' said Steve as Alex got up to leave. 'All I can say is that it's lucky you managed to drum up those extra cash injections. They must have totalled close to a million pounds. We couldn't have survived without it. Isn't it time you let me into the secret? Where did the money come from?'

Kelly's breathless arrival saved Alex from having to reply. 'It's Megaquest.com,' she panted. '… On the phone. Quick!'

Fifteen minutes later, Alex was calling Doug and Sandra into his office.

'I wanted you to be the first to know,' he said gravely and with his eyes cast down. 'I've got some good news and some bad news.'

Doug and Sandra exchanged concerned glances. 'Give us the good news first,' they urged.

Alex could no longer carry on the pretence. His expression turned to one of glee. 'We've got it – we won the Megaquest.com campaign. I want you to know I'm holding you personally respon-sible!'

There were grins and handshakes and slaps on the back. The

Megaquest.com campaign would be one of the largest and longest running in the agency's history. It wouldn't guarantee the agency's longevity – but it would certainly underwrite the immediate future.

Sandra was the first to speak: 'We might have had our differences, Alex. But you're the one to be congratulated around here. This new *Star Trek* approach? … I want you to know that I'm convinced. And I think you've just proved that we can reinvent ourselves.

'And another thing …' she continued. 'You know that collection of art hanging in the corridors? I don't think we need it any more. If you want to sell the lot, that's fine by me.'

Doug looked at Sandra in disbelief. She had personally chosen most of the paintings – and now it seemed that she couldn't care less about them. But Doug switched his attention to Alex. 'I don't like to be a killjoy,' he said, 'but you mentioned there was some bad news?'

'Perhaps the other news is not so bad after all,' replied Alex. 'It's about the art collection … uuh … you know it was worth about a million pounds?'

'*Was?*' asked Sandra suspiciously. She glanced at Doug, then reached to flick open the venetian blinds that curtained Alex's office. Her favourite Rothko stared back at her through the glass.

'Yes,' confirmed Alex with attempted nonchalance, 'I had to sell all the originals – to keep us afloat. I knew you wouldn't mind putting up with these copies for a while. But perhaps we could start to buy the paintings back. I'm sure my friend Dirk could trace them. Perhaps we could acquire one for every major account we win – just like in the old days?'

'Before we discuss that,' said Sandra, 'Doug and I have our own news for you!' She approached Alex with her fingers splayed out. A large engagement ring sparkled at him.

'*Perhaps I went too far with that vision of collaboration,*' thought Alex.

□ □ □

That evening found Alex at home with Sarah.

'Alex, you're making me nervous,' she said. 'Why don't you do something useful, instead of pacing about?'

'I'm just thinking about my contract with DKNU ...' replied Alex. 'As you know, the contract was for only six months. But I'm sure the banks and shareholders will want me to stay on. Yet I'm not sure that would be the best route for me, or for us.'

'Well, it won't help to pace about,' she said. 'It's just like when you kept talking about that VIM formula all the time ...' She paused in thought for a few seconds. 'OK, Alex – here's an idea: why not apply that formula to yourself.'

'To myself?'

'Yes,' she continued. 'Try to write down your vision for yourself; how you are going to keep yourself inspired; how you are going to keep track of your momentum.'

'I guess this VIM formula could apply to a person,' observed Alex. He worked with the idea for a while, and gradually realised where his future lay.

THE VIM OF SELF-LEADERSHIP

Most research shows that leaders think strategically about their own careers.

To be effective over the course of a whole career – rather than merely for the lifetime of a project or the duration of a corporate role – the effective leader applies some form of vision-inspiration-momentum approach to himself.

While some leaders address these issues implicitly, most are explicit – at least with themselves.

- These leaders have a clear **vision** of their ultimate career ambition and the steps and goals along the way.
- They know how to keep themselves and their supporters **inspired**, regularly take the relevant tonics, and even move on from apparently attractive positions if they feel they are stagnating.
- They keep track of their **momentum**, measuring their progress against self-imposed deadlines (and, perhaps less healthily, against the progress of their peers).

The next page suggests questions you should be able to answer, if you are to keep your career on track.

Your future success may arrive in ways you do not yet imagine and cannot plan. But it is said that luck favours the prepared.

THE LEADER'S PERSONAL VIM

VISION
Creating meaning:
Can you describe your career goals succinctly? Do they add meaning to your life and ennoble it? What will be the title of your obituary?

Seeding and testing:
Have you discussed your vision with trusted friends? Have you incorporated any of their views?

Sculpting the skills:
How has your vision helped you identify skills to build?

INSPIRATION
Charisma and trust:
What training or practice would help you project greater charisma? Have you earned the trust of others to help you in career matters? Do you trust others, and your intuition, enough?

Engaging and uniting:
Does your vision engage and unite your passions and interests? Are you just being driven by others' aspirations?

Repeating and reinforcing:
Does your 'self-talk' aid (or impede) your career?

MOMENTUM
Encouraging initiative:
Have you taken enough initiatives and risks with your career?

Galvanising progress:
Do you use your historical achievements as a springboard for further success?

Clearing the way:
Do you remove obstacles – e.g., your dysfunctional traits?

SUPPORT FOR VIM
Urging and celebrating:
Are your goals aggressive enough (or too ambitious)? Do you acknowledge and reward your own successes?

Living the values:
Do you periodically review your philosophy of leadership, and live the values that you espouse?

Corralling attention:
Are your aims known to all who could help you? Do you have the right mentors?

Epilogue

Leadership is as much an art as it is a science. And the spectrum of effective leadership styles is as broad as that of great styles of painting or music.

The pages which conclude each chapter of this book explain techniques employed by most great leaders. By way of analogy, these techniques correspond to the musical notation used by most great musicians.

But the 'true-to-life' story that ran through this book can claim to portray the leadership style of only one fictional individual (albeit a highly typical one).

It seems appropriate, therefore, to account briefly for the shades of emphasis which characterise differing leaders in real life.

Preferred challenges

For reasons that probably relate to deep-seated psychology, some people are more entrepreneurial than others. They relish the challenge of founding new ventures and growing them rapidly.

At the other end of the spectrum, there are leaders who prefer to be dealing with the emergencies and crises that threaten to destroy organisations.

Between these extremes are leaders who prefer to work with an existing organisation, to energise or strengthen it over time.

In being effective, these leaders all create some form of vision and inspiration and momentum in the people who follow them. But the 'products of leadership', which the leader leaves in his wake, will differ in emphasis. For example, the vision promoted by the entrepreneur will more likely relate to a 'quest' than to a 'bible of values'. On the other hand, a leader who has chosen the challenge of reshaping the culture of an existing organisation may prefer the latter basis for his or her vision. Exhibit 1 provides further examples.

Thus, the specific style of a leader is – to some extent – determined by the nature of the challenge to which he or she is drawn.

EXHIBIT 1

THE VARIETIES OF VIM

Leadership type, and best-matched challenge	FOCUS, ACCENT OR FLAVOUR OF VIM:		
	Vision of ...	Inspiration via ...	Momentum through ...
1 Grow the organisation rapidly			
Entrepreneur, *driving expansion of new venture*	The quest	Adventurous spirit	Improvisation, reallocation of scarce resources
2 Energise the organisation			
Evangelist, *(re)fashioning values/ culture*	Enshrining dogma, '10 commandments'	Missionary zeal	Role modelling behaviour, precedent
Politician, *uniting rival factions*	Balance of power	Wise judgement	Reckoning of power, quid-pro-quo rewards
Strategist, *driving strategic initiatives*	Collective foresight, new industry structure	Compelling logic	Key performance measures, acquisition, disposal
Change agent, *driving operational initiatives**	Streamlining, leanness, order from chaos	Challenge to reinvent	Project milestones, external measures – e.g. service levels
3 Deal with emergencies			
Field-Marshal, *responding to crises*	Victory; the enemy, war and priorities	Call to battle	Speed, medals of honour
Surgeon, *retrenching*	Smaller but stronger and more nimble	Salvation by our own hands	Performance against targets

*E.g., customer service, logistics, supply-change management, innovation, learning organisation, post-merger integration.
Note: the last three columns illustrate examples of the leader's emphasis in a given situation, but this is obviously not intended to preclude the use of other listed accents as sub-themes.

Few people can lead in all of these situations, and effective leaders know the extent of their repertoires. They therefore also know their limitations, which are often linked to their broader philosophies of leadership (discussed below). When confronted with situations that lie outside their spheres of expertise, effective leaders typically:

- Engage others who can complement their expertise – either as mentors, or as members of a relevant team, or as partners in the leadership challenge.
- Explicitly view the situation as an opportunity to extend their leadership skills – proceeding more warily than usual, and planning accordingly.

Preferred philosophy
The leader's beliefs and philosophy of life are the second determinant of his or her leadership style. They affect, for example, the ways in which the leader hangs on to control, or delegates. They shape how the leader uses power, or abuses it.

Though this book is not a psychology textbook, Exhibit 2 sets out the most important dimensions along which leaders (or would-be) leaders differ.

Somewhere across these dimensions lies a band that represents an effective mind-set. The position of that band obviously depends on the specific business situation with which the leader is dealing, and on the social era in which he is operating. Nowadays, that band clearly lies to the right-hand side of the chart – though operating at *either* end of the spectrum brings risks that need to be addressed.

To be truly effective in interacting with people and leading them, the leader needs to be consciously aware of his own preferred philosophy (Exhibit 3), and be capable of fine-tuning it when necessary.

EXHIBIT 2

Philosophies of leadership

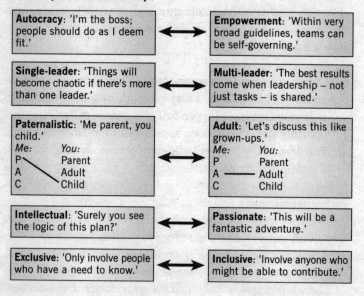

Autocracy: 'I'm the boss; people should do as I deem fit.'	**Empowerment**: 'Within very broad guidelines, teams can be self-governing.'
Single-leader: 'Things will become chaotic if there's more than one leader.'	**Multi-leader**: 'The best results come when leadership – not just tasks – is shared.'
Paternalistic: 'Me parent, you child.' *Me:* *You:* P Parent A Adult C Child	**Adult**: 'Let's discuss this like grown-ups.' *Me:* *You:* P Parent A ——— Adult C Child
Intellectual: 'Surely you see the logic of this plan?'	**Passionate**: 'This will be a fantastic adventure.'
Exclusive: 'Only involve people who have a need to know.'	**Inclusive**: 'Involve anyone who might be able to contribute.'

Take a few minutes to review these dimensions of leadership. Pencil in the profile of your own 'usual' approach.

Of course, the way you lead should be influenced by the nature of the initiative you are leading. (See Landsberg, *The Tao of Coaching*, chapter 10).

EXHIBIT 3
Personal styles

Your leadership philosophy is driven by – indeed, is a manifestation of – your more general personal style. If you have not already had a 'health check' in this area, consider some or all of the following approaches:

1   **Feedback from your peers and 'subordinates'.** If your organisation has not established a way to provide this, use photocopies of the questionnaire in appendix 1 of this book, or the *'Team Performance Appraisal Form'* in appendix 6 of *The Tao of Coaching*.

2   **The Myers-Briggs Type Indicator.** This widely used profiling technique is based on earlier work by Jung, and addresses four aspects of your personality. (See Briggs-Myers, *Gifts Differing*).
    - How you are energised (Extrovert vs. Introvert).
    - What you pay attention to (Sensing vs. Intuition).
    - How you make decisions (Thinking vs. Feeling).
    - How you live and work (Judgement vs. Perception).

3   **Belbin team profile.** This focuses on the role you tend to play in teams. It suggests nine potential roles, which include Plant, Shaper, Completer, Team worker, Specialist, Co-ordinator, Resource investigator, Implementer and Monitor evaluator. See Belbin, *Team Roles at Work.*

4   **FIRO-B profile.** This measures Control, Inclusion, Affection, Interpersonal skills and Expression of anger. See the work by Schultz cited in the Bibliography.

Appendices

Appendix 1

Leadership profile and aspirations

Mark your current profile and aspirations out of 10 on each question. Plot your current leadership profile (and your aspirations) on the facing page.

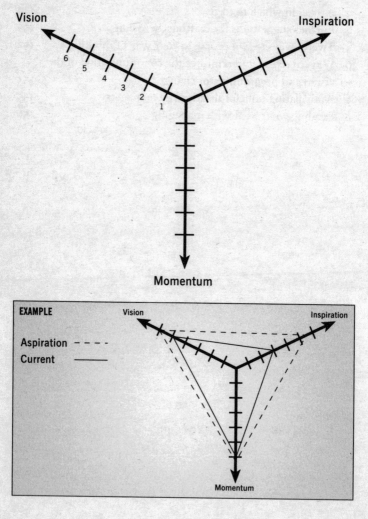

VISION

Current Aspiration

__ __ Regularly develop novel ideas, grounded in facts

__ __ Express ideas 'indelibly', creating meaning for others

__ __ Have the courage to express a 'draft' vision of change

__ __ Incorporate others' ideas into the vision

__ __ Identify the impact of your ideas on the organisation's skills

__ __ Ask others to test the practicality of the vision

__ __ Totals ▶ Divide by 10 ▶ Current __; Aspiration __

INSPIRATION

Current Aspiration

__ __ Convey passion and conviction in presenting ideas

__ __ Personally live the values implicit in the proposed way forward

__ __ Draw on a broad repertoire of styles in engaging others

__ __ Unite opposing factions, when needed

__ __ Use multiple forums for reinforcing your message

__ __ Include and embrace others – not exclude, nor alienate

__ __ Totals ▶ Divide by 10 ▶ Current __; Aspiration __

MOMENTUM

Current Aspiration

__ __ Redefine crucial accountabilities, when needed

__ __ See the 'critical path' for implementation, and levers to pull

__ __ Aim for 'early wins', and publicise them

__ __ Enshrine proven innovations into the *modus operandi*, fast

__ __ See and remove the main obstacles to others' progress

__ __ Convince others of genuine urgency – but celebrate, too

__ __ Totals ▶ Divide by 10 ▶ Current __; Aspiration __

Appendix 2

Typical traits of effective leaders
The following traits are frequently identified when describing leaders. Clearly, not all leaders possess all traits!

Driven:	Courageous:	Engaging:	Upbeat:
Ambitious	Active	Charming	Cheerful
Assertive	Adventurous	Empathetic	Enthusiastic
Committed	Bold	Good listener	Happy
Competitive	Confident	Humble	Hopeful
Conscientious	Daring	Passionate	Humorous
Decisive	Physically fit	Pleasant	Optimistic
Disciplined	Proactive	Sensitive	Positive
Dominant	Restless	Social	
Energetic	Risk-taking	Solicitous	
Focused		Vulnerable	
Goal-oriented			
Hard-working			
Initiative-seeking			
Productive			
Tenacious			

Source: Boyett & Boyett, *The Guru Guide* (with amendments)

Wise:	Balanced:	Principled:	Charismatic:
Aware	Adaptable	Consistent	Credible
Conceptual	Flexible	Constant	Eloquent
Creative	Grace-under-	Dependable	Inspiring
Curious	pressure	Direct	Motivational
Far-sighted	Mature	Fair	Mysterious
Intelligent	Moderate	Firm	Spiritual
Smart	Patient	Loyal	Visible
Understanding	Pragmatic	Open	
Visionary	Responsible	Reliable	
	Sensible	Respectful	
	Stable	Trustworthy	

Appendix 3

Arenas in which to focus

Effective leaders are highly focused. They know which arenas they should channel their leadership energies into. Obvious though this may sound, it is a lack of this focus that often prevents aspiring leaders from realising their full potential.

EXAMPLE

Imagine you're the newly elected leader of a major law firm. How will you spend your time in this new role?

For some of the time, you will *not* be leading. You'll he representing the firm externally, or dealing with continuing cases for some of your clients. But what about *leadership?*

As a brilliant strategist, you'll be tempted to participate heavily in establishing whether the firm should diversify into new areas. But this would be a mistake. You'll end up managing the project, rather than leading the firm. Your time is probably better spent in cajoling other partners to oversee the project, based on their ability to contribute, the credibility they will bring, and the obstacles which you can avoid by including them.

The arena in which the leader creates vision, inspiration and momentum depends partly on the size of the team he is leading:

Culture –
e.g., create the values that foster departments collaborating work together in designing new products

Process –
e.g., revamp the process for reviewing new products

Substance –
e.g., lead a team to design a new product

Leading small team

Leading large organisation

As leaders are promoted, they need to guard against embroiling themselves in too many detailed issues, at the expense of attending to issues of culture.

EXERCISE

Review your current slate of major initiatives. Are you spending too much time on issues of detailed content – work that you could delegate? For initiatives that you are leading, are you creating vision, inspiration and momentum?

Appendix 4

Further suggestions for crafting the vision

Criteria	*Comment*
A dynamic story ● Responsive to the organisation's history and needs ● Grounded in market facts, insights and foresight ● Offering a better tomorrow	**Not:** 'We're going to create more economic value than any other Fortune 500 company – follow me.' **Rather:** As in all good stories, include the historical frame of reference, as well as the future one. 'Once we were *xyz*, but then *xyz* happened, which resulted in *xyz*. But I foresee *xyz*; so we shall *xyz*, and we know we can make it – though we can expect *xyz* trials along the way.'
Complete (at least impressionistically) ● Focused on specific changes needed ● Highlighting the priorities, and inclusive of the steps needed ● Linkable to measurable goals	**Not:** 'We're going to get a can of Fiz'R'U within arm's length of everyone on the planet (but you guys around the world will each have to figure out how to do it).' **Rather:** As in all good stories, ensure that the plot is convincing, that the sub-plots articulate well from the main plot, and that the climax of the adventure is conclusive. But the audience isn't interested in every minute detail of the action and characters – the challenge is to portray *only* the essential highlights.
Laden with meaning ● Providing meaning to people's (work) lives, inspiring them to achieve their personal best ● Appealing to higher values	As E. M. Forster observed in *Aspects of a Novel* 'the king died, and then the queen died' is not a story. 'The king died and then the queen died *of grief*' **is** a story. Tap into the power of emotions as you develop the vision; portray people, not just assets.
Memorable ● Novel in reframing or providing perspective ● Summarisable in a short tag-line	Remember the film *Jaws*?

Refer to McKee's *Story*, or Forster's *Aspects of a Novel*.

Suggestions

- Review analyses of the organisation; test widely

- Get data; consult experts

- Scan widely to stimulate your boldness and creativity

- Check by asking selected listeners to paraphrase the implications

- Review the vision through 'half-closed eyes': ask if the main points are still apparent. Check you've addressed the journey, not merely the destination
- Ask 'How will we know when we've arrived?'

- Check that the vision works for you; check that it portrays *people* – not just assets

- Read (or hear on tape) speeches by great leaders*

- Use – or consider – similes, analogies and metaphors

- Beg, borrow, steal, brainstorm

*See, for example, MacArthur (editor), *The Penguin Book of Historical Speeches*.

Appendix 5

Twelve ways of winning people to your way of thinking*

1 The only way to get the best of an argument is to avoid it.
2 Show respect for the other person's opinions. Never tell people they are wrong.
3 If you're wrong, admit it quickly and emphatically.
4 Begin in a friendly way.
5 Get the other person saying 'yes, yes' immediately.
6 Let the other person do a great deal of the talking.
7 Let the other person feel that the idea is his or hers.
8 Try honestly to see things from the other person's point of view.
9 Be sympathetic to the other person's ideas and desires.
10 Appeal to the nobler motives.
11 Dramatise your ideas.
12 Throw down the challenge.

---

*Excerpted from Dale Carnegie, *How to Win Friends and Influence People*.

Appendix 6

Ways to repeat and reinforce the communication of the vision and programme for change

Direct action by the leader:
- For 'routine' management meetings, radically refocus the agenda.
- Personally intervene in those decisions which will have highly visible results:
  - Promotion of managers
  - Transfer of managers
  - Staffing of important projects
  - Activities during management 'retreats'.
- Pinpoint specific aspects of the changes needed (e.g., Carlson's 'Moments of Truth' outlined in chapter 10).

Indirect actions, encouraged by the leader:
- Change the curriculum of training courses.
- Change the written criteria used during recruitment interviews (which reinforces messages in the minds of the interviewers).
- Change the physical layout of offices, reception areas and other 'community space'.
- Set up new institutions (e.g., the 'Hamburger University' established as a training facility by McDonald's).

Words spoken by the leader:
- In meetings that have been especially convened.
- As part of previously established meetings – e.g., salesforce conference.
- During informal discussions.

Words written by the leader:
- In the company newsletter.
- On the company intranet.
- In external media (if it will be seen by employees).

Appendix 7

Anticipating unhelpful actions by managers

Possible obstructive action	Pre-emption
Failing to free up (sufficient) people to work on the agreed initiatives – reluctance to volunteer their people, not delivering for start-up, 'clawing back' time for their department's own projects.	Give advance warning, and obtain early 'cast-iron' guarantees of resources.
Undermining pilot programmes (possibly to impede their broader rollout) – e.g., by prejudging the results, or by spreading false rumours about their ineffectiveness.	Communicate unambiguously and indelibly to the primary audiences in the organisation.
Continuing to model or require 'old' behaviour, not 'new' behaviour – e.g., stifling rather than promoting new values such as entrepreneurship.	Obtain visible 'sign-up' to the new approach in public forums; take actions that dramatically symbolise the new approach; provide training or support if needed.

In both pre-empting and/or correcting these behaviours, refer to the strategies indicated in 'Engaging and uniting' (chapter 9, page 51), and 'Power and influence' (chapter 20, page 117).

Appendix 8

Leading contrasted with managing

Distinctions in terms of 'VISION':

Manager	Leader
Does things right	Does the right thing
Focuses on the present, the short term and the bottom line	Focuses on the future, the long term and the horizon
Seeks order	Relishes change
Contains risks	Takes risks
Appeals more to reason than to emotion	Appeals to both emotion and reason

Distinctions in terms of 'INSPIRATION':

Manager	Leader
Uses control	Relies on trust
Structures the team and organises it	Engages people and aligns them to the new direction
Applies incentives	Inspires
Appeals to 'official' approach	Appeals to common cause
Emphasises structure, tactics and systems	Emphasises core values, shared good and philosophy

Distinctions in terms of 'MOMENTUM':

Manager	Leader
Targets efficiency	Focuses on effectiveness
Asks 'how, when?'	Asks 'what, why'?
Administers	Innovates
Optimises within narrower constraints	Skirts rules and policies, or has them changed
Exercises positional authority	Uses personal influence

Bibliography

STRONGLY RECOMMENDED

Campbell, J, *The Hero with a Thousand Faces*, Fontana Press, London, 1993
> The foremost expert on myth presents the archetype of the hero's journey – some aspects of which will inspire the mortal leader.

Kipling, R, *If*, Penguin Books, London, 1977
> If you approach this poem with leadership in mind, it will amply repay your (re)reading. Also at www.di.unipi.it/~coppola/if.html

Kotter, J P, *John P Kotter on What Leaders Really Do*, Harvard Business School Press, Boston, 1999
> An excellent, practical, concise portrayal of the leader's role. If you read only one book from this bibliography, this should be it. Part 1 is *Leadership and Change*. Part 2 is *Dependency and Networks*.

FULL BIBLIOGRAPHY

Adair, J, *Effective Leadership Masterclass*, Pan Books, London, 1997
> Illuminates principles of leadership with reference to Julius Caesar, Alexander the Great, Napoleon, Florence Nightingale and others.

Belbin, M, *Team Roles at Work*, Butterworth Heinemann, Oxford, 1993
> A presentation of Belbin's widely used approach, which includes nine roles (e.g., Plant, Shaper, Completer-Finisher).

Bennis, W, *On Becoming a Leader,* Addison-Wesley, Reading, Mass., 1989
> An insightful perspective by pioneering leader and behavioural psychologist.

Bower, M, *The Will to Lead*, HBS Press, Boston, 1997
Subtitled 'Running a Business with a Network of Leaders',
this book comes from the man who founded and shaped the
world of management consulting, and who led McKinsey &
Co for nearly three decades.

Boyett, J H and Boyett, J T, *The Guru Guide*, Wiley, New York,
1998
Succeeds in demystifying the terms, concepts and theories of
top commentators on management.

Briggs-Myers, I, *Gifts Differing*, Consulting Psychologists Press,
Palo Alto, California, 1992
Presents the Myers-Briggs Type Indicator – widely used to
profile personality types, and based on Jung's earlier work.

Carnegie, D, *How to Win Friends and Influence People*, Pocket
Books, New York, 1994
A classic. Its suggestions have stood the test of time – selling
more than 15 million copies since 1938.

Covey, S R, *The Seven Habits of Highly Effective People*, Simon &
Schuster, London, 1992
Extols both Private Victory (Be proactive, Begin with the end
in mind, Put first things first) and Public Victory (Think
win/win, Seek first to understand then to be understood,
Synergise), and Renewal (Sharpen the saw).

Crainer, S (Editor), *The Ultimate Business Library*, Capstone
Publishing, Oxford, 1997
An excellent synopsis of 50 top books on management, with
useful perspectives on their authors.

de Bono, E, *Lateral Thinking*, Penguin Books, London, 1990
An aid as you dismantle obstacles and clear the way for
progress.

Dunne, P, *Running Board Meetings: tips and techniques for getting
the best from them*, Kogan Page, London, 1997
Includes help on motivating top managers in the crucial
setting of the board meeting.

Forster, E M, *Aspects of the Novel*, Penguin Books, London, 1974
A classic of literary criticism that will help some leaders to
make their 'vision' compelling.

Gardner, H, *Leading Minds*, HarperCollins, London, 1996
   The man who revolutionised our understanding of
   intelligence and creativity in such books as *Frames of Mind* and
   Creating Minds now does the same for leadership.

Gardner, J W, *On Leadership*, Free Press, New York, 1990
   Reaches for the 'issues behind the issues' in leadership: shared
   values, social cohesion and renewal of the institution.

Garratt, R, *The Fish Rots from the Head*, HarperCollins, London,
   1997
   Clarifies the tasks and liabilities of the board, and provides a
   programme of learning.

Harvard Business Review, *On Leadership*, HBS Press, Boston,
   1998
   Eight of *Harvard Business Review*'s most influential articles on
   leadership, from 'The Discipline of Building Character' to
   'Whatever Happened to the Take-Charge Manager?'

Katzenbach, J R and Douglas, K S, *The Wisdom of Teams*,
   HarperCollins, London, 1994
   Gets to the essence of teamwork (in its many guises):
   performance results, collective work products and personal
   growth – through skills, accountability and commitment.

Katzenbach, J R and the RCL team, *Real Change Leaders*,
   Random House, New York, 1995
   Focuses on the crucial role of middle managers as change
   agents.

Kozubska, J, *The 7 Keys of Charisma*, Kogan Page, London, 1997
   In search of that elusive quality, this work focuses on
   confidence, vision, communications, style, 'moving and
   shaking', visibility and mystery/enigma.

Landsberg, M, *The Tao of Coaching*, Profile Books, London,
   2003
   Tools and techniques for boosting your own effectiveness at
   work by inspiring and developing those around. In the same
   format as the book you are now reading.

Landsberg, M, *The Tao of Motivation*, Profile Books, London,
   2003
   Practical suggestions on how to motivate yourself and others.

Law, A, *Open Minds*, Orion Publishing, London, 1998
  The co-founder of an acclaimed advertising agency tells the story of how his team built a model corporation for the twenty-first century.

Levicki, C, *The Leadership Gene*, Pitman Publishing, London, 1998
  Advice on developing a lifelong career in leadership. Presents a taxonomy of leadership styles.

MacArthur, B (Editor), *The Penguin Book of Historical Speeches*, Penguin Books, London, 1996
  Includes speeches by Lincoln, Robespierre, Gladstone, Nelson, and the classical orators. A companion volume presents twentieth-century speeches.

Machiavelli, N, *The Prince*, Penguin Books, London, 1961
  Though common parlance has tarnished the author's name, even the altruistic leader can learn much from this considered treatise on leadership.

Maister, D, *True Professional*, Free Press, New York, 1997
  Focuses on the professional services firm: serving clients, teamwork and leading the firm.

McKee, R, *Story: substance, structure, style and the principles of screenwriting*, Methuen, London, 1998
  The book's subtitle says it all. From a recognised doyen of writers' coaches, a definitive work to help the leader develop his 'vision'.

Nanus, B, *Visionary Leadership*, Jossey-Bass, San Francisco, 1992
  Focuses on that 'v' word, aiming to help you create a 'compelling sense of direction for your organisation'.

Northouse, P G, *Leadership – theory and practice*, Sage Publications, London, 1997
  Describes and analyses a wide variety of theories of leadership.

Pfeffer, J, *Competitive Advantage through People*, HBS Press, Boston, 1994
  Includes excellent examples of how leaders and managers have challenged past practices and achieved extraordinary success.

Pfeffer, J, *Managing with Power*, HBS Press, Boston, 1992
In Tom Phillips' words, Pfeffer does a masterful job of demystifying and deSatanising the topic of power in organisations.'

Phillips, D T, *Martin Luther King, Jr. On Leadership*, Warner Books Inc., New York, 1999
Though not written by the civil rights leader himself, the author nevertheless characterises well King's demagogic style of leadership. Includes illuminating excerpts from King's many speeches.

Rosen, R H, *Leading People*, Penguin Books, London, 1996
Eight principles of leadership (vision, trust, participation, learning, diversity, creativity, integrity and community), each illustrated by four case studies.

Rupert, A, *Leaders on Leadership*, (Private printing*), 1967
Brief comments on leadership by 42 leaders from many countries. Includes 'Creativity in Banking' by David Rockefeller. (*Reprint of a lecture to the Institute of Business Administration at the University of Pretoria.)

Schultz, C, *FIRO: a three-dimensional theory of interpersonal behaviour*, Holt, Rinehart and Winston, New York, 1955
The original presentation of a technique for assessing leadership, which is widely used in business (and beyond).

Senge, P, *The Fifth Discipline*, Random House, London, 1992
This classic work proposes that the learning organisation adopts five disciplines (systems thinking, personal mastery, mental models, building of shared vision and team learning).

Strage, H M (Editor), *Milestones in Management*, Blackwell Publishers, Oxford, 1992
A unique collection of original seminal articles that have helped to advance management thinking. Includes seven articles on leadership – including works by Maslow, Drucker and Herzberg.

Ulrich, D, Zenger, J and Smallwood, N, *Results-Based Leadership*, HBS Press, Boston, 1999
Focuses on leadership for results in four areas: Employee, Organisation, Customer and Investor.

Acknowledgements

I thank heartily the following people for sharing their insights into leadership, and for contributing substantial vision, inspiration and momentum to this book:

- Danny Bejarano – Executive Chairman, Omnipack PLC
- Susan Bloch – Director, Executive Coaching, Hay Management Consultants
- Helge Bokenes – Director, Orkla Brand School
- Partha Bose – Director of Marketing, Monitor
- Ben Cannon – Director of Training and Development, Goldman, Sachs & Co
- Jerry Connor – Managing Director, Bridge Management Training Ltd
- Ian Davis – Managing Director, McKinsey & Company, UK
- John Heatly – formerly Director, J. Walter Thompson
- Victoria Holt – Columnist and broadcaster
- Eva Indra – Author
- Dr Petros Kalkarnis – Managing Director, Gillette Europe
- Olivia Landsberg – Broadcaster
- Ruth Tait – Vice President, Korn Ferry/Carre Oban
- Harry Langstaff – formerly Brigadier, the British Army; Partner, McKinsey & Company
- Lucinda McNeile – Editor
- Julian Seaward – Partner, McKinsey & Company

I also thank for their support: Martin Liu and Penny Daniel at Profile Books, HIGGINS (my cartoonist), Sophie Sassoon and David Godwin.

Summary and every-day checklist

Effective leaders take action under *each* of these headings, *every day*. Use a photocopy of the following page to help you do the same.

1 **Focus.** Are you leading in the correct arenas? Or killing yourself by meddling where others should lead? Or shying away from command you should assume? *Chapters 3, 17, 18*

2 **VIM.** Are you building Vision *and* Inspiration *and* Momentum? Or merely employing your strongest of these three suits? *Chapters 1, 2, Epilogue*

3 **Promised Land.** Have you painted the vision of the goal as an indelible and graphic image? Or merely relied on facts and figures and decrees? *Chapters 5–7*

4 **On balconies.** Are you continually appearing on the right balconies? Or are there important constituents to whom you are currently invisible? *Chapters 8–10, 14, 16*

5 **Honeycomb.** Even if you've selected the relevant teams, are you urging them (and helping them) to take bold imaginative initiatives? *Chapters 4, 11–13*

6 **Power.** Are you amassing power and influence, and exercising them responsibly? Or assuming you can lead without them? *Chapter 20*

7 **Reins.** You've delegated – but have you abdicated? *Chapters 18, 19*

8 **Hot buttons.** Are you taking actions which others will see as highly symbolic and important? Or merely churning out the same old memos? *Chapters 15, 21*

9 **KPIs.** Does everyone know the new Key Performance Indicators – and are you monitoring them? *Chapter 16*

10 **Show you care.** Are you spending at least 90% of your time face-to-face with people? Have you decimated the time you spend on 'admin'? *Chapters 3, 17–21*

Leadership actions for week of: _____

	To do
Focus	
VIM	
Promised Land	
On balconies	
Honeycomb	
Power	
Reins	
Hot buttons	
KPIs	
Show you care	

Index